Rx FOR HAPPINESS
AN OB/GYN'S STORY

FOR HAPPINESS
AN OB/GYN'S STORY

By

MARVIN H. TERRY GRODY, M.D.

Lombard Press

Rx for Happiness: An OB/GYN's Story

Published by Lombard Press

For further information, please contact Jeffrey G. Grody
Phone: 860-232-6200
Email: grodyj@comcast.net

Cover design by Tami Feldman

Book layout by Arbor Books, Inc.
www.arborbooks.com

Printed in USA

Rx for Happiness: An OB/GYN's Story
Marvin H. Terry Grody, M.D.
1. Title 2. Author 3. Memoir

Library of Congress Control Number: 2008906246
ISBN 10: 0-9795212-1-1
ISBN 13: 978-0-9795212-1-8

To my wife, Sue,
whose patience, understanding and counsel were integral to the heart and soul of my dedicated and consuming career.

FOREWORD

In August, 2000, I was privileged to interview Dr. Terry Grody on *The Today Show*. We discussed advances that he pioneered in treating pelvic prolapse and incontinence, debilitating conditions that afflict many older women. Then 78 and in his 54th year wielding a scalpel, Terry radiated the passion and exuberance of a young resident, coupled with the sagacity and compassion of a man who has helped countless patients for more than half a century.

Now retired, Dr. Grody has recorded the highlights of his career as an obstetrician-gynecologist in a collection of short stories that I know you will enjoy as much as I have. Tales dating back as far as 1949 reveal a skilled, creative and caring physician—the kind all of us would want as our own. His stories show that the fire within Terry when I interviewed him seven years ago was ignited decades earlier and blazed throughout the years to the delight and benefit of his patients.

Fortunately for all of us, the flame still burns brightly today and Terry has preserved this memoir as a testament to a most remarkable career!

Katie Couric
March, 2007

CONTENTS

INTRODUCTION

It's been a ball! Drama, humor, pathos, challenges, emotions, ideas, tensions, tears of joy, tears of sorrow, laughs, sobs, triumphs—all sorts of interesting and exciting people—life at its fullest. I could not have chosen better, and if given another chance, I would do the same thing all over again. I was born to practice medicine, specifically obstetrics and gynecology. Medicine was part of me from the start and it has remained my endless passion, endowing me with memories rich beyond imagination.

I became enthralled with the prospect of a medical career at the earliest age. Growing up in Hartford, Connecticut in the 1920's, my dad, George Everett Grody, was my first hero, for all the usual devoted and loving reasons. He had arrived in the United States in 1899 from a shtetl in the Ukraine, a two-year-old immigrant with penniless parents, and the influence of his personality and impeccable character left its mark on me forever. My second hero, discovered at the age of three, was our family physician. Here was a man revered by all, as were all medical practitioners at that time. Held in awe throughout the community, doctors enjoyed top billing among their fellow men in those early days of the twentieth century. To me, it was all so simple. Doctors dealt with the health and welfare of their fellow human beings. Everybody else worked in services or with materials, which, from my youthful vantage point, seemed nowhere near as important.

Also, in the days before World War II, doctors came to the patient's house, which enhanced their aura of apparent omnipotence. You got sick, you called the doctor, and he made a house call to see you with his little black bag, his stethoscope, and his prescription pad. The doctor's office, in comparison, was far less often visited. Doctors owned automobiles. Many middle class families had none. Transportation principally was by trolley. So, the doctor came to you; you did not go to the doctor.

Prior to the doctor's arrival, the house would be made immaculate. Only clean, freshly laundered towels were exposed, together with a new bar of soap. Coffee or tea would be available if the doctor needed a break. We watched for his arrival through a front window. The front door would be opened before he had a chance to ring the bell. The doctor was greeted like royalty and he would act the part.

Whether you had just a common cold or a little diarrhea, the routine of questioning and thorough exam—eyes, ears, nose, throat, skin, heart, lungs and abdomen—was always the same. You were bound to get your money's worth. All this occurred in front of the family, standing by with hands clasped in silent reverence. It was high drama in the bedroom marked by such commands as, "Say ah," and "Take a deep breath." Then came the prescriptions, almost always two, truly euphemistic placebos, but I thought they were magical potions, bound to make the patient well. No matter what, after the doctor's visit the patient recovered! Sensational, I thought.

Such experiences occurred with regularity. In the 1920's, we were still almost two decades away from antibiotics, and upper respiratory infections and digestive tract afflictions (lumped generally into a category known as the grippe) were rife. An average family of 4-6 members would experience 5-6 house calls per year from its family practitioners. (Many families used a pool of three doctors, taking whoever was available at the time of need.) So it was that I was afforded ample opportunity to formulate vital opinions about these portentous individuals who, it seemed to me, played such a critical role in keeping us out of life-threatening trouble.

I had the ultimate respect for those who could work such miracles. There could be no greater gift than to possess the secret knowledge of how to cure disease. Little did I know, or did any of us realize, that almost all of the remedies physicians typically prescribed in those days were useless (fortunately harmless) and that, with few exceptions, we would get well in spite of the doctors. From my vantage point, physicians were like gods. At the age of four, I made a definitive statement to my father, "I am going to be a doctor."

My drive toward that goal never wavered but my reasons changed. As I matured, I saw that becoming a physician could present me with a lifetime of challenges. I would never be bored and each day would be more exciting than the day before. I could not imagine a more fulfilling or gratifying career. Also, as a naturally gregarious individual, I relished the prospect that, as a practitioner, I would be working with people all the time.

Thus, my original reasons for pursuing a career in medicine were, I must admit, essentially selfish. That fellow human beings might benefit from the good job I would do was strictly incidental at the time. I wanted to enter the field of medicine because that was where I would be happiest.

When I was accepted to the University of Pennsylvania School of Medicine in 1943, my dad was bursting with pride. His education had carried him only as far as high school. I not only had successfully completed college, but would be receiving a graduate education as well. I would now show him the best I could to justify all that he had given me.

Starting with my first day of medical school on April 4, 1943, and continuing all the way to this, my 85th year, it has been a marvelous adventure. Each year has been more exciting than the one before, all catalyzed by my decision to pursue a career in medicine. I have delivered more than 5,500 babies, some in dramatic circumstances. I have enjoyed the privilege of either performing surgery or lecturing in 24 states, as well as Canada, Singapore, England, France, and Turkey. I have become acquainted with dozens of famous people, both in and out of medicine. I have published a textbook, produced a record number of surgical educational films, and been interviewed on national television. I have received major awards as a distinguished gynecologic surgeon. Most of all, as a result of my work, I have been able to make significant and memorable contributions to the lives of my many patients. I feel extremely fortunate.

My story ends with a twist. After dedicating my life to caring for others, I suddenly and dramatically found myself on the receiving end of life-saving medical care in late December 2004. As detailed in the last chapter, I experienced first-hand the emotional trauma of a desperately ill patient who is forced to place ultimate trust in his or her physician under terrifying circumstances. I was very fortunate to survive my encounter with death and to add the perspective gained from that experience to my understanding of the leap of faith patients make when they entrust themselves to their physicians' care.

Not so fortunately, however, my late-2004 medical experience forced me to curtail what had been a busy schedule as Professor of Obstetrics and Gynecology and Senior Gynecologic Consultant at Cooper University Hospital in Camden, New Jersey. With newfound time on my hands and the opportunity to reflect not only on my extremely satisfying career as a physician but also on my final act, in the role of patient, I have documented several dozen vignettes that, to me, illustrate why physicians are the most fortunate people on earth. All of the stories are true and are related exactly as they occurred, although I have changed most names and left out a few insignificant details in the interests of protecting patients' privacy.

In obstetrics and gynecology I did, in fact, find the lifetime of challenge and fulfillment I sought. Looking back, I am astonished by the varied array of experiences and the multitude of emotions and life lessons they generated. I originally wrote these accounts so I could share them with family and friends, but I was widely encouraged to publish them.

I hope you enjoy reading them as much as I did living them.

Marvin H. Terry Grody, M.D.
Philadelphia, Pennsylvania
March, 2007

Chapter 1
Elizabeth, the First

"I did not come to Hartford to die," she laughed to the reporters as she lovingly cuddled her newborn babe, "And I never dreamed that ice cubes had any value beyond cocktail parties." How easy it was to talk about it now that it was all over. All she really had wanted was a baby. She did not bargain for a death-defying adventure along the way.

To their delight, Barbara and Charles (aka Sam) Kilner had conceived at the end of May 1957. They could not have been happier. Sam had just been promoted within the IBM Corporation from his post in Detroit to the position of general manager of IBM's New England operations, headquartered in a handsome new building on the corner of Woodland Street and Asylum Avenue in Hartford, Connecticut. Their home was but five blocks away on Farmington Avenue, which happened to be just two minutes from my office and ten minutes from Hartford Hospital. This ebullient and charming young couple had embarked on a seemingly idyllic life of marital hope and happiness. I was the lucky doctor to be drawn into this serene picture by virtue of a referral from Dr. Andrew Veldhuis, a residency partner of mine who had opened a practice in Detroit after we had finished our training together in St. Louis a few years earlier.

While under my care, in just my fourth year of practice, the Kilner pregnancy had blissfully matured without any unusual challenges. Suddenly, like a dynamite blast from nowhere, on Friday morning, January 3, 1958, everything changed dramatically into what would evolve as both a desperate and historic triumph in medical annals. The full story, as told by feature editor, Ralph Minard, would ultimately consume all of page three of the February 28, 1958 edition of *The Hartford Times.*

But, as the newspaper story would subsequently state, the thrilling story is best appreciated by starting at the beginning. Mrs. Kilner, age 28 and in the eighth month of pregnancy, had virtually never experienced a headache. On that fateful Friday morning, however, she called my office to report a severe headache, worse while lying down, slightly relieved when erect. I was reached at the hospital, where I was finishing work on another case. I instructed her to meet me at the office at once.

I examined Barbara and inventoried the ordinary complications of pregnancy, discarding each one. This obviously was unusual. Headaches at that stage of gestation could be caused by toxemia of pregnancy but there was absolutely no evidence of toxemia. I knew she had no history of chronic or intense headaches. I took into account the suddenness of the occurrence and the severity of the headache. I felt it was important that the pain was only on the left and noted the appearance of a few vague positive right-sided neurological signs.

My brain, through the recall of experience, was now signaling a diagnosis. Once while in my post-internship days at the 98th General Hospital in the U.S. Army in Germany and again during my residency training at the Barnes Hospital in St. Louis, I had seen cases of ruptured cerebral aneurysm in pregnancy. Both patients had died with the infants they were carrying. A review of the medical literature when I was in St. Louis revealed no history of any survivals of this relatively rare complication.

"Sam and Barbara, something very serious may be going on here," I told them with due candor. "Barbara needs to be hospitalized and diagnostic tests must be started at once. Leave directly for the Hartford Hospital emergency room. I'll have one of my internist colleagues waiting at the door for you. The admitting office will have been alerted to your arrival. I'll be down there shortly to be with you. One thing I'm sure of; whatever is happening is incidental to the pregnancy. In other words, the pregnancy itself is fine." That was the best reassurance I could give them. "Be prepared for immediate blood tests and x-rays. A spinal tap will be the most important thing. I will see you down there. Get going."

They left. I turned to Faith Henry, my chief aide and office manager, with tears filling my eyes. "I sent her down to the hospital to die."

She watched, aghast, as I dialed the hospital switchboard to page Dr. Wetstone, who responded a few moments later. "Howard, I need you desperately. What are you doing right now?" I asked.

"We just finished a long morning's rounds and I'm munching a donut with coffee. What's up?" he queried.

"Finish your munching quickly and hustle your butt over to the E.R. to greet Barbara Kilner, a seven-months-pregnant patient of mine. Now you are not going to believe this—she'll be walking in on her own power, escorted by her husband, but my diagnosis is ruptured cerebral aneurysm."

"Ha, ha, ha," he mockingly responded. "How does an obstetrician come up with such a rare diagnosis? And she's still conscious?"

"Howard, I'm dead serious." I quickly filled him in with all pertinent details. "Please, pursue my diagnosis first and foremost. I'll bet my house on it. She will go into a coma shortly. I prepared them for a stat spinal tap. I'm sure it will be loaded with blood."

"Alright, I believe you."

"Waste no time. Perhaps we can save her—it would be a first. Alert Scoville, anesthesia, and the O.R. I'll talk with the admitting office."

I turned to Faith, "Cancel all my appointments for today. I'll be down there with Barbara. Maybe, with an early diagnosis, this will be the one case where we can at least save the baby."

A cerebral aneurism is the ballooning of a weakened artery or vein in the brain. The wall of the blood vessel distends and is prone to rupture, sooner or later, causing a hemorrhage into the brain, most likely terminating in death. Hope in these cases, such as there is, rides on early diagnosis and a small leak so that the bleeding is slow.

It didn't take long for Howard Wetstone to call back. "You are absolutely right!" We did the tap with the neurology guys almost at once after the Kilners got here. The spinal fluid was loaded with blood, just as you predicted."

"What else?" I asked.

He described multiple abnormal neurological signs showing up on the right side of Barbara's body. "So we know the aneurism is on the left side of the brain," I said. That is how the neurologic system works. My anxiety and impatience were sizzling, "Where is Scoville? Is anesthesia setting up? Is the O.R. aware?'

"Calm down," came the retort. "Scoville is on his way down

and should be here within minutes. We are moving like crazy."

"How is Barbara responding?" I asked.

"She is beginning to fade out, as we would expect."

"And is Sam right there?"

"We are keeping him fully informed. He is sitting patiently right alongside Barbara."

"Tell him I'm on my way down."

Dr. William Beecher Scoville was a brilliant neurosurgeon. No one on the Hartford Hospital medical staff was more respected. He enjoyed a national reputation and had been President of the American Society of Neurosurgeons. I had known him since my days as a rotating intern at Hartford Hospital in 1947. My deep regard for him as a demanding and dedicated super-doctor developed in that time and had continued to grow. I just knew there could be no one better to take charge of Barbara's destiny.

I caught up with Sam at the hospital. He urged me to talk directly with Barbara's mother, widow of a former chief of otolaryngology at Harper Hospital in Detroit. I did this at once, explaining in no uncertain terms the extremely dire nature of her daughter's condition. Without even speaking to Sam, she demanded that we put Barbara on a plane to Detroit at once. I stopped her cold. "You are being irrational. She is in a potentially life-threatening state. Even if there were an airline that would risk carrying her, you would best have a long pine box waiting at the airport, not a stretcher. Barbara could not be in better hands than she is in right now. Get yourself to the airport for a flight to Hartford." And so she did.

I caught up with Bill Scoville. He had reviewed the flow of events up to his arrival on the scene and had conducted his own physical examination. He also had called in our skilled radiologists for diagnostic input and a cerebral angiogram had been performed. This is a special x-ray study that outlines the blood vessels of the brain and which can localize blood vessel problems. The torn aneurysm was found at the base of the left side of the brain on the same level as the left ear and slightly ahead of it.

Barbara was given appropriate pre-operative medication under the close observation of a team of anesthesiologists. The operation on Barbara's brain to stem the bleeding and eliminate the aneurism was set to begin as soon as an adequate level of hypothermia had been reached.

Hypothermia is a state of lowered body temperature in which blood flow through the body is significantly reduced by forcing the body temperature to drop from the normal 98.6 degrees Fahrenheit to approximately 82 degrees. Although this feat is accomplished today by sophisticated electronic means, in 1958 it was achieved by sheathing the body in ice from head to toe.

Attaining this level of hypothermia is a valuable technique in operations where the surgeon is working around tissue of extremely vital and delicate nature such as that of the brain. Hypothermia reduces the oxygen requirement of brain tissue to 25 percent of its normal needs without tissue impairment. Three hours of tedious pre-operative preparation were required for the medication to take effect and for Barbara's body to cool sufficiently.

Our pre-operative preparation was monitored via telephone by the neurosurgical team at the Hospital of the School of Medicine of the University of Montreal. This group, the members of which were former colleagues of Dr. Scoville, enjoyed an international reputation as leading experts in clinical research on cerebral aneurysms. Bill Scoville felt that consultation with these Canadian physicians in this treacherous medical situation was critical to his efforts to achieve the best possible outcome. At his request, they gave detailed advice, including appropriate surgical maneuvers. In his typical professional manner, he wanted absolute certainty that nothing was omitted in the management of this case. The Montreal doctors expressed envy that Barbara was not in their domain. They badly wanted to be the very first doctors to announce a triumph in this kind of case.

At no point did anyone lose sight of the primary objective, saving the life of the mother and, hopefully, preservation of all her normal mental and physical functions. We also were desperately concerned with what effect all this activity, particularly the internal cooling, would have on the unborn child.

Where was I during all this time? I had changed into operating room attire shortly after arriving at the hospital. Then, I had picked up a scalpel from the O.R. and clutched it in my hands while I remained within touching distance of Barbara until long after the neurologic surgery was concluded. Since sudden death was, unfortunately, possible at any time, I was alertly prepared to snatch the unborn babe in a matter of seconds if circumstances required.

The operation took more than three hours. The skull was opened and the ruptured blood vessel located. It was in a branch of the chain of arterial vessels at the base of the brain known as the Circle of Willis. With meticulous care so as to avoid any direct damage to cerebral tissue, metal clips were placed on the afferent (supply) side of the torn artery to dramatically terminate the hemorrhaging. Suddenly, as the operation was being completed, the patient burst into extremely severe laryngeal spasm, resulting in forced labored breathing of such magnitude that the blood pressure could be pushed high enough to dislodge the clips. With lightning speed, Scoville resolved the situation by performing a tracheotomy (incision and tube placement in the neck), bypassing the larynx. It was a life-saving move.

As *The Hartford Times* recorded, I remained with Barbara Kilner for 26 hours without sleep. I speculated that it must have been the longest stretch of time ever for holding a scalpel ready for action, without using it even once. Finally, eight hours of undisturbed sleep were the reward for my vigilance. Luckily, the stork did not come to visit any of my other patients during that time.

Mrs. Kilner, the world's first known survivor in these circumstances, then spent the next three-and-one-half weeks in the hospital convalescing. A series of tests relevant to mental capability were all within the normal range. Doctors claimed her recovery was complete not only mentally but physically as well. Multiple serial cerebral angiograms revealed no further vascular disturbance. Electro-encephalographs reflected normal brain wave patterns. The neurologists and neurosurgeons were delighted!

The pregnancy seemed to be totally undisturbed by all the fuss. I was delighted! But we still had fingers crossed.

So what about the next event, the delivery, hopefully to unveil a healthy baby? There was no way to disguise the collective anxiety of the Kilners, myself, and all the other doctors. Because he was fearful still of any derangement of the brain arterial clips, Dr. Scoville recommended delivery by cesarean section in order to avoid possible significant blood pressure elevations during an active hard labor.

Thus it was, on Valentine's Day, 1958, at thirty-nine weeks of pregnancy and an estimated fetal weight of eight pounds, that we prepared Barbara Kilner for section. General anesthesia, wherein the mother is put to sleep, was not thought to be a wise choice in this case, particularly from the fetal perspective. Regional anesthesia, like a spinal or epidural, was the best option.

It was not to be. The anesthesiologists had no difficulty entering the intradural space in the spinal canal but could only obtain sporadic effects over the abdomen and pelvis. They concluded that there was marked disruption of the usual even distribution of the anesthetic agent in the spinal fluid as a result of adhesions formed from the massive bleeding from the ruptured aneurysm. Obviously, a spinal was not going to work. In 1958, epidural anesthesia was new on the scene and, as expert as they were, our anesthesia people were still learning how to work it with no luck with Mrs. Kilner. A caudal anesthetic, similar to an epidural only lower down, was entertained as a further alternative, but no assurance of a better result was forthcoming. Besides, the patient was fed up with needles being stuck in her back and pleaded for an alternate anesthetic route. So, as though this case had not already endured enough challenges, the patient and her medical team now faced this new problem, which our anesthesiologists were not readily solving. For certain, no surgery was going to begin without anesthesia.

With all alternatives exhausted, I announced, "I will do the section under local anesthesia," to the consternation of all the medical personnel, not to mention the patient. No one had any experience with this approach. Fortunately, this technique had been part of my OB/GYN training as a resident at the St. Louis Maternity Hospital in the Barnes Hospital group at Washington University in St. Louis.

I explained in detail to Barbara, who would be under very mild sedation, how I would inject copious amounts of Xylocaine progressively in four separate layers, from the skin of the abdomen inward through and including the peritoneum covering the uterus. I reassured her, with great patience, but ultimately convincingly, that she would feel us at work but with no pain. Only in the fifteen seconds it would take me to extract the baby from the uterus would she feel tension and discomfort. Immediately afterwards she would be put to sleep under general anesthesia while I made the appropriate closures.

Needless to say, there were several curious onlookers to observe the first cesarean section ever performed at Hartford Hospital under local anesthesia. The case went exactly as described, without a hitch. Barbara was a stalwart patient and was rewarded with a healthy female babe who immediately was named Elizabeth by one who was probably the world's most anxious father at that moment. Neonatologist-pediatricians on hand declared Elizabeth to be normal in every respect. Emotion was rampant. The ordeal was finally over. Tears of joy flowed freely from everyone except Barbara, who was peacefully asleep.

Over subsequent months and years, through a variety of tests, no residual mental or physical deficiencies were ever demonstrated from the aneurysm in either mother or child. Elizabeth graduated later from the University of Vermont where, perhaps not coincidentally, she developed skiing expertise. As the "kid who came in from the cold," could it not be said that she had had better preparation than average for skiing weather?

Three years after the ruptured cerebral aneurysm, Barbara Kilner returned to me for a repeat cesarean section at Hartford Hospital, despite having moved to North Carolina in the interim. Elizabeth was joined by a brother. "I was not about to change my luck," Barbara proclaimed.

This most remarkable case, so glowingly reported in *The Hartford Times*, was duly recorded in the neurosurgical literature for all time as the first of its kind. Indeed, Elizabeth Kilner was first in many ways but she will always be first, above all, in my memories.

Chapter 2
My First Hysterectomy, Catalyzed by a Furnace

The tears were rolling down her cheeks as she climbed onto the examining table. The 73-year-old widow could no longer contain herself after imparting her tale of woe.

Proud, indomitable, always cheerily boastful of her independence till now, Emily White felt whipped for the first time in her life on that cold mid-December morning in 1951 in St. Louis, Missouri.

The Barnard Free Skin and Cancer Hospital, an affiliate of the Barnes Hospital Medical Center, stood but eight city blocks from the rooming house owned and managed by Mrs. White and on which her livelihood depended. Yet, today, the eight blocks seemed like eight miles. The agony that tormented her short walk to the hospital was the direct result of a fourth degree prolapse of pelvic organs that had literally broken loose during the previous month from long-term weakened supports. She had been informed one week earlier that her condition was not amenable to a pessary and that only appropriate surgery would solve her problem.

So why the tears in this tough lady who never let anything get her down? Certainly it was not the need for surgery—she could handle that. Then came the answer. "Who will take the ashes out of the furnace each morning and shovel in a new batch of coal to keep my place heated for my roomers?" she lamented to me as I recorded her history that winter morning. (Homes were still commonly heated by coal in 1951.) Little did this lovable senior lady, suddenly more lovable than ever, at least to me, realize that she was telling her sad story to the most eager second-year OB/GYN resident in America, who just happened to possess strong coal-shoveling arms.

In the OB/GYN residency program at the St. Louis Maternity Hospital and Barnes Hospital, four months of the second year called for a rotation through the Barnard Free Skin and Cancer Clinic. In that period, we were inundated with all manner of malignancies of the female reproductive system. However, about ten percent of the surgery addressed benign conditions as a matter of convenience for neighborhood women. Such was the situation with Emily White, who did not have cancer.

Mrs. White was isolated socially. Her two children lived in California with their own families and had not maintained a supportive relationship with her for 25 years. All her friends had either passed away or were themselves too disabled to be of meaningful assistance. She had no one to cover for her if she became confined and/or restricted.

Dr. Bill Natoli, the senior resident, examined Mrs. White with me and confirmed that she indeed required extensive pelvic surgery, including a vaginal hysterectomy. I informed him immediately of the practical difficulties involved in Emily's circumstances, and before he could ponder more than a moment, I volunteered that I would solve this poor women's dilemma by taking responsibility for the furnace management and ash removal over the requisite two weeks of confinement and restricted activity. Bill grinned widely and said, "If you're going to do all that, she's yours." I was in heaven!

Five days later, we brought Emily White, properly prepared, to the O.R. where I, also properly prepared after four nights of intensive academic review, embarked on my very first major surgical adventure. Under the guidance of Dr. Natoli and Dr. Andrew Brundage, our faculty preceptor for the day, I joyfully and meticulously engineered a vaginal hysterectomy, bilateral salpingo-oophorectomy and complete anterior and posterior vaginal repair in slightly over three hours. It could not have gone better.

While Mrs. White enjoyed a rapid and uneventful recovery, I paid all the required conscientious post-operative attention to the patient, her furnace, and her ashes.

My elation as a budding healer knew no bounds. Like a kid, I called my parents in Hartford to relate my new status as a full-fledged gynecologic surgeon. I considered my Barnard rotation a burning success.

Chapter 3
Face the Problem

My examining hand moved inward, slowly and gently. The index finger fell into a hole. Uh, oh, what's going on? I knew this was not the anus because my external exam easily ruled out a breech presentation, revealing a vertex (baby's head) into the pelvis. I wiggled my fingers around and discovered a protuberance adjacent to the hole. Suddenly it came to me. This was a mouth and nose configuration. My goodness, I was dealing with a face presentation! Then I found the jaw—it was stuck in the hollow of the sacral curve. What a dilemma! My jaw dropped.

This was October 1949, and I had just started the fourth month of my OB/GYN residency at the Barnes and St. Louis Maternity Hospitals. This was my turn for out-patient community-home delivery. Today, almost 60 years later, it's hard to believe that a prestigious, leading medical institution in a major, modern city was still sponsoring home deliveries in the mid-twentieth century, but it was so for at least four more years after my encounter with the practice.

The unusual arrangement between the hospitals and the

community provided for up to three projected deliveries per month for indigent women living within two miles of the hospital. Of course, they had to be in good health. An additional stipulation was the presence of one or more young children in the household for whom there would be no one to care in the patient's absence. The assignment for home delivery was based on a rotation system involving the first-year residents. A battered but working Ford coupe was available in the rear parking area of St. Louis Maternity Hospital to transport the resident physician, an R.N., a student nurse, and sterile equipment when the call signaling the onset of labor in one of the designated patients came through.

Thus was I situated with my nursing team at the home of Maggie Smith, who was in strong labor and confronting me with the very uncommon and serious dilemma of a face presentation in a mentum posterior position. Because the mechanics of such a circumstance, i.e., the infant's jaw locked into the hollow of the sacral curve, made it impossible for a vaginal delivery, cesarean section would be necessary. If the jaw were in an anterior position, vaginal delivery could be effected. We knew that removal of the patient by ambulance to the hospital L&D (labor and delivery) unit was mandatory because delivery at home was clearly untenable. The patient was militantly opposed to hospitalization, however. I had zero experience with face presentations. We were trapped and was I ever apprehensive to find myself in this predicament!

With little alternative, I came up with a crazy idea. Maggie had experienced two previous easy deliveries of babies weighing well over eight pounds, so I knew I had enough room for reasonable manual manipulation. The cervix was almost completely dilated and the vertex had descended almost to mid-pelvis. Maggie was willing to tolerate significant discomfort if it meant avoiding the ambulance trip and hospitalization. I was going to attempt rotation to an anterior mentum position, which would permit vaginal delivery. I had never heard of this before, but it seemed logical.

I proceeded first with appropriate local anesthetic injections. Then I wrapped my left hand gently around the baby's face. Slowly and steadily, with each contraction, I turned the jaw a fraction more forward. The nurses were monitoring the fetal heart tones through a fetoscope. It took almost an hour but we did it. The anterior rotation was a success!

Twenty minutes later the lusty cry of a healthy newborn female with the most edematous face on earth resonated across the room. Mutual congratulations were extended by everyone. We had come through. We packed up our stuff and drove back to the hospital in a festive mood. As required, I wrote up my account of the case for the record, embellishing the report with a bit of what I deemed to be well earned self-congratulation.

Two weeks later, I was summoned into the office of our OB/GYN chairman, the widely revered and beloved Dr. Willard Allen, whom everyone addressed as "Professor" out of respect for his monumental discovery of progesterone. He laid me out with as rough a scolding as this affable gentleman was capable of delivering.

"You broke the rules. You know that lady belonged in the hospital. You had no experience and you acted foolishly," he admonished. He did not mince words.

I sheepishly agreed with all that he said but in the end, with considerable audacity, I asked, "Professor, I was wrong but, in all truth, what would you have done in my situation?"

He clearly had not expected such an impertinent question. After a few moments of thoughtful silence, however, he grinned and said, “I probably would have done the same thing, but don’t tell anyone I said that.”

At Maggie Smith’s six week postpartum checkup, she brought with her as pretty an infant girl as you could find anywhere in St. Louis that day.

Chapter 4
Homage to Boxer Shorts

"And don't forget—on the way home, you must stop at a men's clothing store to pick up a dozen pairs of boxer undershorts. On arriving at home, your first move will be to trash your drawer full of briefs; you will never wear that style again." Can you imagine a weirder way to address the husband of my very first patient in private practice? Obviously, there has to be an explanation for such a command issued in March 1953, before I had even set up an office.

Seven months away from completing a wonderfully rewarding OB/GYN residency in St. Louis, I was laying the groundwork for a practice upon my return home to Hartford. I was approaching my 33rd year and had yet to begin making a living. I had no money. I would need a friendly banker. Somewhere in the background of my thoughts I probably needed a wife. Above all else, for anything to work, I needed patients, and my first one was already in place.

I had met Margaret Roberto and her husband in December 1952, at their home in Windsor, CT, just outside of Hartford. It was my first trip back to initiate arrangements for an office. A friend of my family, a neighbor of theirs who had heard of my special interest in infertility, had referred the Robertos to me. Good friend that he was, he had told the Robertos that I was a hot shot with all the up-to-date techniques on becoming pregnant when a problem existed, emphasizing that I had already co-authored three published scientific papers on the subject.

The Robertos, though not specifically targeting pregnancy, had not used any method of contraception for two years. By now they were acutely aware of a possible problem. They believed they had been sufficiently active to conceive by now. They wanted some answers and some action, and they wanted no delay. "Why wait till you open your office?" they had asked by telephone in November. I told them I would be back in Hartford in December and again in March to complete arrangements for opening my office on July 1, 1953.

So it was that, one week before Christmas, I was gathering the medical history of Margaret and her husband, Michael, in their living room. I had brought sufficient equipment with me from St. Louis to permit me to conduct a physical exam at the same time, and this I did in the bedroom. Margaret, Michael and I covered all the necessary explanations and instructions that are integral to an initial infertility appointment. I made out orders for laboratory tests and arranged for the most important test of all, a semen analysis.

When I returned in March, I performed a hysterosalpingogram, which revealed a normal endometrial (uterine) cavity and fallopian tubes. I had prearranged to do this in a radiology office of an acquaintance from my old intern days at Hartford Hospital. The review of the basal temperature charts displayed a textbook series of perfectly standard ovulatory patterns. Everything in this case, including the examination, the history, and the tests, was well within normal limits except for the semen analysis.

The semen actually was perfectly normal in amount, color, and consistency, and yielded adequate numbers of normal-appearing spermatozoa except for their motility, which was distinctly sluggish. This prompted me to search out the one aspect of the history I had omitted, the type of undershorts worn by the husband. Interrogation to this effect showed that he consistently wore briefs, even at night in preference to pajama bottoms. "Aha," I thought. Perhaps now I had stumbled on the answer to the problem.

My training in infertility had brought me into contact with studies showing that subjecting the scrotal sac to even minimal increases in temperature could produce a major negative effect on fertility in a small but significant segment of the adult human male population. Briefs pull the scrotum up against the male perineum, where the environment is warmer than that in which a free-hanging scrotum exists, as with boxer shorts. In the St. Louis infertility group at Barnes Hospital, two couples had achieved conception where the only positive tactic we pursued was the underwear change in the husband from briefs to boxer shorts. Following the change in underwear, the Robertos, by my order, deliberately avoided attempting conception to allow time for physiologic adjustment by the scrotum to the new environment. Then, on July 3, 1953, just two days after my official entry into practice, I performed a follow-up semen analysis in my mini-laboratory. The motility of the spermatozoa was superb! They were racing all over the slide.

A specific coital schedule surrounding the projected ovulatory phases was then devised for the Robertos to follow, to which they adhered religiously. Margaret missed her period in October. The basal temperature remained elevated. Success! At 40 weeks, to the joy of a considerably extended family, many of whom subsequently became patients, I delivered a lovely female infant. Of incidental note, she grew up to be a United Airlines hostess and became a patient of mine herself.

As for Margaret, in 1956 she presented a second child, a healthy male infant, to the world. At a time when mothers of newborns typically lamented the odiferous task of cleaning soiled cloth diapers, Margaret instead gave a silent blessing of thanks each time she placed a load of laundry containing Michael's boxer shorts in the washing machine.

Chapter 5
Good Night and Good Luck

Six years, multiple doctors, many tests, a variety of plans, prayers galore, and no pregnancies. Their friends had at least one, even two, children already, and all the Coopers had were empty dreams, no luck. They were not happy.

I was new in practice. I had an office, brand new equipment, a receptionist-aide, a telephone, a big debt at the Riverside Bank and Trust Co., and only one patient. I was back in Hartford, perhaps the biggest small town in the U.S.A.; but it played out like a small town. I had loads of old friends. They knew I had been a top-flight student and, therefore, might be a top-flight physician. But I was single and a ladies' doctor. My old friends were not rushing to send their wives to me, not in 1953 in Hartford. I needed a lucky break. Then it happened.

In 1953, there was only one local physician specifically targeting his medical practice toward infertility. The subspecialty of reproductive endocrinology was still 20 years in the future and most OB/GYN practitioners of the time were content with cut and dried work like routine pregnancies and abdominal hysterectomies for fibroids. No one was interested, it seemed, in the patience, time requirements and uncertain results that were the basic elements of infertility workups. Besides, relatively speaking, the monetary return for the temporal requirements was low. So the time was just right for me, with training in infertility and plenty of time on my hands, to hit the jackpot.

There was one catalyst that broke things open for me. One year before my return to Hartford as a practitioner, Dr. John Leonard, the Director of Graduate Education at Hartford Hospital, had invited me back, as a former intern now in the last year of my residency, to lecture on infertility at Grand Rounds. That turned out, ultimately, to be a springboard launching me on my way because other physicians came to dump their infertility problems in my lap. That was how the Coopers found their way to my office. I was their "last resort" but they were my big chance. The Coopers were immensely popular and their childless dilemma was known far and wide. I felt that if I could crack this case, the world would be mine.

A more forlorn couple I had never seen. My initial contact with the Coopers in my office was particularly tense because Ellen had known me from childhood and seeing me again for the first time in years under these dark circumstances was obviously complicating her emotional turmoil. Ellen and I had spent our early childhood in the same neighborhood in Hartford. She had followed a few grades behind me all the way from kindergarten through high school. I now met Rick for the first time.

I greeted Ellen and Rick as warmly as I knew how and with as welcoming a smile as I could drum up. We wasted no time getting down to business. It did not take long for the anxious couple to realize that they had finally stumbled on someone genuinely interested in adopting a formal, organized and scientific approach toward overcoming their infertility problem. Initially, we went over in detail their rather haphazard experience up to that moment. They felt they were getting no real help, just good wishes accompanied thus far by unsubstantiated assurances that, since they seemed normal, pregnancy would happen in time with a little patience. Their frustration had grown by leaps and bounds with each passing fruitless month. "Making love has become joyless, especially since, one after another, our friends get pregnant at will. Then we hear all the happy tales about the fun they are having with their kids. We surely are happy for them but it's killing us to see what we're missing."

It was easy for me to sympathize with this very affable couple. I went over all the physiologic details of achieving conception, explaining that everything in their picture pointed to a successful conclusion. I was as reassuring as I could be, asserting that all that was necessary was a fresh start, a strongly positive up-beat attitude and belief in themselves.

And, I didn't mention, a few simple tricks that I would throw in. I was going way out on a limb, but there was no other choice. Although they did not know it, I was about to ask these two fine, innocent people to embark on a psychological scheme that I could only hope would work and which carried no guarantees. Did I have a right to chance possible total failure in view of their dismal experience to date? My answer to this self-imposed question was a decided "yes!" There was nothing to lose and everything to gain. They were at wit's end and it was time to go for broke.

"Here's what we're going to do. We will start from scratch. All previous tests, plans, advice, and agendas must be obliterated from memory. They never existed." I gave them a few seconds to absorb this strong statement. Then I sprang the real shocker on them. "For the next three months you will practice deliberate contraception. You will enjoy sexual activity as though you were newly married, using condoms on every occasion."

Before they had time to challenge or protest, I encouraged them to smile at the apparent contradiction inherent in my proposition and to contemplate how wonderful it was to be freed from the pressure associated with an endeavor in which they had lost all confidence. I broke out in a grin, compelling them to join me. "Now this is the plan. You will take 400 mg of vitamin E each morning, remain on a sensible diet, engage in daily exercise, and return here in three months prepared to start a family. Nonsense is over!" Ellen and Rick were astounded. After two hours of earnest and tense dialogue, they were different people from the two sad sacks they had been at the start. Hope suddenly loomed for the future.

Only I knew that I had sold them a bill of goods based solely on prayer and luck. What about the vitamin E? It was strictly a ploy. I had to introduce at least one new element to physically identify a new course. Both the Coopers and I had been exposed to a concurrent onslaught of advertisements on the multiple health "virtues" of vitamin E. So it was a timely psychological maneuver that could do no harm.

During the next three months, I telephoned them twice to see how they were doing and to let them know I was thinking about them. You bet I was! The course of my future was as dependent as theirs on the success of this treatment.

The time was up. We outlined Ellen's next projected ovulatory phase on the calendar. This was easy since her menstrual cycle was as regular as clockwork. I spotted precise isolated times for ejaculation. I encouraged the Coopers to continue engaging in sex for pleasure, sans condoms, playfully explaining that, as a general rule, they could hang from the ceiling during coitus, if they wished, but the missionary position was mandatory during the ovulatory phase of her menstrual cycle. Finally, after reviewing how Ellen would record her daily basal temperature to demarcate ovulation, I threw my final two instructions at them. In each of the three planned ovulatory ejaculating episodes, a pillow was to be placed under the junction of the buttocks with the thighs to exaggerate the normal female pelvic tilt. Secondly, the first two male thrusts at ejaculation were to be made at deep penetration followed by completion of the action at a slightly withdrawn distance. In this way, the initial 2-3 drops of ejaculate, known to contain almost all of the spermatozoa, would be removed from dilution by the balance of the ejaculate and the penis would not be disposed to displace the spermatozoa outwardly. The Coopers were enthralled; no physician had previously offered such precise and logical advice. Their enthusiasm was palpable.

As they prepared to leave, I gave them, in jest, my last advice. "Be sure to listen regularly to the reports of Edward R. Murrow of CBS on Channel 3. When he gives his 'Good Night and Good Luck' sign-off, take it personally, as though he means it just for you."

Guess what! They made it! My wild gamble paid off. The basal temperature remained elevated well beyond the usual length of Ellen's menstrual cycle and menses did not occur. Early breast signs of pregnancy were apparent by 20 days after ovulation. A pregnancy test would have been redundant.

As incredulous and ecstatic as the Coopers were, and as much as they wanted to shout their gleeful news from the rooftops, they recognized that good sense begged patience till time had gone beyond the danger zone of miscarriage. Actually, Ellen decided that she would inform her parents at the end of the first trimester and let the rest of the world catch on from her first appearance in maternity attire.

Well, that's how it happened. Word roared through the charming couple's wide circle of friends like a prairie fire on a hot summer day. Suddenly people began to ask about Dr. Grody and "his magic touch." I reveled in the publicity. I had reached the level of credibility and respect I was after. They could label me a genius, if they wished. I was not about to tell anyone that the happy event was nothing more than the chance combination of a little psychological trickery and an abundant helping of good luck.

Ellen Cooper enjoyed a normal gestation culminated at term by delivery of a healthy daughter. Two years later, with no psychology or tricks, she gave birth to a son. But that's not the end of the story. Several years after the second child, she had "an accident" that produced child number three. How about that for a complete fairy tale turnaround? All three lived happily ever after.

Chapter 6
Immersion

How wrong they were!

"Don't let them get to you." "Their problems can eat you up." "You'll be caught in situations with no release." "Guilt feelings will creep all over you."

This kind of misdirected advice and so much more like it was being fed to medical students in the first half of the 20th century by academic physicians across the U.S.A. The format being preached was one of non-involvement; that doctors should treat medical challenges "objectively" and remain aloof from all intervening family or social problems.

Consider that such advice was coming from practitioners working in the cloistered atmosphere of an institutional and consulting setting, quite dissimilar from the environment associated with medical practice out in the community, peopled by physicians with ongoing attachments to patients and families. Counsel of this nature was fine for general surgeons who would enjoy very short-lived patient relationships, as with appendectomies, hernia repairs, or gallbladder surgery, but absolutely not for the general practitioner, internist, obstetrician, or gynecologist, where prolonged, often lifetime, associations with whole families were the rule.

In the mid-twentieth century, it simply was not possible for a primary care physician to remain uninvolved and aloof. Contrary to the ill-conceived advice of the academics, I not only found it impossible to escape intimate involvement, for me it was an integral ingredient in the joy of practicing medicine. I have always regarded the practice of medicine as a privilege unequaled by any other in human livelihood, one that could be engaged with pure passion, offering rewards of accomplishment not attainable through any other pursuit.

Many of the anecdotes reported in this book took place in an era when the doctor-patient relationship was generally more intimate and trusting than is often the case today, and when thoughts of malpractice and negligence were on the very back burner. That time, now gone, stands in stark contrast to the atmosphere of recent years in which medicolegal confrontations between patients and physicians occur with alarming frequency.

Another difference was that, when my career began, doctors practiced by themselves or in partnerships of two doctors only, totally unlike the large, less personal group practices that emerged steadily over the last two decades of the 1900's. Today's larger practices tend to be run like businesses under often confusing, complicated, and constrictive formats labeled as managed care or health maintenance organizations. These formats have led to insurance-dictated decisions regarding medical care that physicians often feel are not in the best interests of the patient.

My own style as a physician was well suited to those earlier days. Back then, insurance plans did not pay for office visits and only partially covered doctors' fees for hospital services. I never charged a penny for service to the wives of clergymen or to members of physicians' families. I charged reduced or negligible fees to friends. I considered it a privilege to care for them and I was flattered that they chose me as their physician. For trivial matters involving loyal patients of long standing, I often waived my fee. In hardship cases, I found alternative methods of payment, such as lobsters for the pregnancy care of a seafood merchant's wife, chickens for the care of a farmer's wife, and original paintings twice from young artists.

I loved the practice of medicine, specifically obstetrics and gynecology. I was fortunate never to feel the pangs of "burnout," a syndrome that is claimed to affect 30-70% of obstetrician-gynecologists these days. For me, working with people and for people, teaching other doctors new and better surgical techniques, and innovating and creating with my colleagues were all singular joys that I was extremely privileged to experience throughout my career. I always felt "it could never be better than this."

Chapter 7
Bobbie and the Good Samaritan

Waving my arms frantically, I had popped out of my stalled car and raced to the middle of the road. Desperate, I had to flag down the next vehicle to come by. In a matter of moments, a blue Chevrolet screeched to a halt but a few feet in front of me. An astonished priest at the wheel could not believe this strange start to his day of worship. Thus began my warm and wonderful friendship with Father Gengras at 6:10 A.M. on Sunday, September 16, 1962.

At 4:45 A.M., my answering service had awakened me to call Mrs. Cohen who thought she might be in labor. I dialed at once and Norman, Bobbie's husband, responded with a description that certainly sounded like early labor. Next, Bobbie picked up and verified the impression. In the office, just two days earlier, the vertex had engaged the pelvis and the cervix was effaced (flattened and shortened). I recalled with her the relatively short labor she had undergone the last time, with Emily. "Get on your horse and waste no time. I'll be right behind you."

I jumped out of bed, brushed my teeth, raced through my shower, tossed on my clothes, and I had my car rolling in a matter of minutes. I would easily make it to the delivery room while they were admitting and preparing Bobbie.

My wife, Sue, and I had become close friends of Norman Cohen, a distinguished professor at a local university, and his wife, Bobbie. The acquaintance began when Sue and Bobbie were introduced to each other at an art exhibit. As couples, we found much in common and they had accorded me the privilege of delivering their first two children, both healthy daughters. Bobbie was not just a patient but also a prized and dear friend and I hoped that I would be able to present Norman with a son.

I was zipping along, entering Hartford from West Hartford on the Asylum Street hill just above Scarborough Street when the motor simply gave out for no obvious reason. I glided to the curb and pumped the pedal. No response. My heart sank. I could not let Bobbie and Norman down—there was no way I could miss this delivery. I needed an angel.

The priest had no wings but he surely filled the bill. Thoroughly puzzled, he hastily absorbed my urgent tale and beckoned me into the car. "What great luck for you and Mrs. Cohen," declared Father Gengras happily. "I'm driving directly across town, right by Hartford Hospital, on my way to Mass in Wethersfield."

With all due alacrity, my newfound clerical savior, whom I was soon to know better, deposited me at Hartford Hospital, where I went in to deliver Bobbie Cohen, "in the nick of time," of a healthy son in answer to his father's prayers.

Needless to say, Father Gengras included Bobbie in his prayers that fateful morning and she and I have included him in ours many times since.

Chapter 8
Blood

She just kept bleeding from everywhere. Stopped in one place, it started up somewhere else. I had never seen anything like it. I was already over three hours and two units of blood into my morning surgical case. "Ninety minutes at most and I'll be out of there," I had figured. "Piece of cake." It just wasn't in the cards, not for a hot shot like me, I thought, to run into trouble on what was so obviously a routine case. Or so I thought. And then I had my come-uppance.

It began in February. Jane Mortenson, at 42 years of age and following three previous vaginal deliveries, presented in the office with a subinvoluted uterus and a history of intractable disabling menorrhagia (heavy bleeding with her periods) and pelvic inflammation. An abdominal hysterectomy was indicated and should have been performed within the next few weeks. Her life was already in turmoil, however, as a result of the unanticipated relocation of her husband's job to western Massachusetts. The accompanying complicated arrangements, she said, would force her to wait till late September before she could return to Hartford for the required operation.

Although not exactly happy with the delay, I had our office

manager call the Hartford Hospital admissions office and operating room for the appropriate scheduling. Jane promised to take heavy doses of dietary iron supplements and to eat a diet replete with elements to combat anemia from vaginal bleeding. She also promised that if the bleeding got out of hand before September, we would go ahead with the surgery earlier regardless of her logistical difficulties. Such a change proved to be unnecessary, however.

Usually a careful planner, I have always made certain that operations were scheduled on days and at times when there would be no conflict with other obligations, except for this single instance. With such a time gap, February to late September, and knowing of no conferences I would be attending in September that year, how could there be a conflict, I reasoned.

In mid-August, peeking at my calendar for the next several weeks, I spotted Jane Mortenson's operative date and my jaw dropped. She was scheduled for the first day of Rosh Hashanah. How could I have let that happen?

There was no way the date could be changed. Despite an already loaded agenda into November, I could still make appropriate rearrangements for a new operating day, but Jane had locked herself in with her own and her husband's work alterations and coverage. I was quite distraught.

I came up with a solution. I would make certain that Jane's case would be on for 8 A.M., the first time of the day, and I would be able to ditch the O.R. at about 9:15 A.M., leaving the well-experienced senior resident to close the abdomen in standard fashion. I then could race off to meet Sue at the synagogue. Both the day and I would be saved!

But here I now stood, going on noon, ensconced in blood, at wit's end. What was I to do! Then I had an idea. I packed the entire operative field with wet cotton sponges and told my assistants to exert steady pressure. Next, I just pulled myself away from the operating table, held my hands out in front of me, turned my face to the ceiling, and exclaimed, in pleading tones, "Alright already! Enough, I will never do it again."

I returned to my place at the operating table and almost in unison, the resident, intern, and nurses asked, "What was that all about?"

"If I told you, you would not believe it," I responded.

We continued the pressure for five minutes with no further movement and essentially no talking, but I think more than one person in the room was praying. Then, slowly, one at a time, we removed the sponges. Astonished, we observed only the barest trickles of bleeding. After signs of relief all around, and a few more touches with the electrocautery needle, we closed without incident.

That evening Sue, in holiday spirit, unwittingly served up Bloody Marys to start off dinner. Was this a divine gesture as a final reminder of my misdeed?

Jane Mortenson recovered from her surgery quickly and smoothly. The pathology report revealed only benign tissue.

I swear to God, this is exactly as it happened!

Chapter 9

An Unusual Journey: From a Salami Sandwich to a Moving Train

"Okay, everybody. Someone is smelling up the place with salami. Who is it?" I hollered out between the second and third sessions while teachers were changing classes.

"It's the new kid with the crutch," came a voice from the back of the room.

Sheepishly and apologetically, the new kid acknowledged he was to blame.

"How come you're bringing sandwiches anyhow?" someone else asked.

This was the first day of school in September 1932, at the height of the Great Depression in one of the fifth grade classrooms of the Northwest Grammar School in Hartford. We were pretty good kids and generally liked each other. We enjoyed school and came to realize at an early age the importance of education. Decent jobs were relatively scarce, going mostly to people who had attended college. Many fathers were out of work. Young as we were, the rampant nationwide poverty of the time had etched its way indelibly into our comprehension. Everyone longed for a better life and many of us had our sights set on college as the way to get there.

The lower schools did not have cafeterias at that time. City budgets could not afford them and many children would not have been able to use them anyway for lack of funds. We all lived within 10-15 minutes walking distance from the school, however, so we were able to go home for lunch in the one hour between morning and afternoon classes, except for Jack Horwitz, the new kid whose family had moved into the district during the summer just past.

There were no "working moms" in 1932. There were hardly enough jobs for the fathers. Mothers stayed home to care for the house and for their children at breakfast, at lunch, and after school.

It only took a few minutes for us to learn that Jack was a surviving victim of the dreaded poliomyelitis, known more commonly at that time as infantile paralysis or polio. He was far more fortunate, though, than our next President, who could never walk again after his bout with polio. Jack was on crutches now while recovering from corrective foot surgery to overcome residual defects from the paralytic illness. His prognosis was good, borne out later by his proficiency at tennis.

We all wanted to help this new kid as much as we could but only on his promise, since he could not walk home and had to bring sandwiches with him for lunch, that never again would he permeate our classroom with odors from salami. He heartily agreed and, on this vow, he and I became friends for life. We would remain inseparable.

But the story does not end here. Jack married Ethel in 1955 and they leaped into pregnancy at once. It was a singularly emotional moment for me when Ethel and Jack marched into my office to entrust her to my care. This was friendship in full blossom. I could claim no greater privilege.

Ethel's pregnancy was serene. Her estimated date of confinement was May 27, 1956. On May 17, an examination revealed an engaged fetal vertex, as could be expected, with a cervix just beginning to efface but still closed. She would probably deliver on time or a few days late. Almost certainly she would wait till I returned from Chicago.

Three months earlier, I had taken and passed Part One, the written section, of my OB/GYN Board Certification exam in New Haven. I was on track for the oral part, the second and last section, on May 20 in Chicago at 11 A.M.

Sue was the mother of one child and we had just embarked on our second gestational venture. Earlier that year, two major domestic plane crashes had killed over 200 passengers.

"You will travel to Chicago by train," she had declared. "There is no way I will chance being a young widow with two babies and no money."

So I went to bed on the evening of May 18, a light suitcase packed and a train ticket for Hartford departure at 9:05 A.M. All set to go. A colleague would cover my practice till my return on the 21st.

The telephone rang. It was 12:15 A.M. Ethel was in labor. I could not have been less happy. The odds were against me. Would I dare leave and have her delivered by someone else? It was a no brainer. I would take Part Two of the exam next year; the train ticket would be a memento. The last thing I wanted was to postpone certification for a year, but I kept my priorities in order.

So off to Hartford Hospital went Ethel and Jack. Ever the optimist—she might, as unlikely as it seemed, deliver in time—I dressed, grabbed the suitcase, and followed them by cab, not my car, with my train ticket in my pocket.

Jack and I sat by Ethel as she labored along. She promised to do her best to meet my travel agenda, but we all knew that she came first. Comply she did, however, with excellent contractions and remarkable progress. The vertex was almost at the pelvic floor by 6 A.M. Both the father-to-be and the honor-bound obstetrician were cheering the patient on her way like two guys at a college football game. Ethel was following her childbirth-training program to a tee.

At 7:25 A.M. the cervix was fully dilated. The vertex was beginning to crown at 7:45 A.M. We moved Ethel into a delivery room where I administered a pudendal anesthetic block. At 8:11 A.M., Lee, weighing 7 pounds 11 ounces, was delivered over a small midline episiotomy which was "duck soup" to close.

I hugged Ethel. I hugged Jack. I literally jumped into my street clothes. I tore down the four flights of stairs three steps at a time in simulated slalom style. At the hospital entrance a taxicab was unloading and I hopped in almost before the last passenger was out. I waved a big bill in front of the driver's eyes. There would be no time to make change. The cab moved as though it had wings.

At Union Station, I flew out the door before the car completely stopped. It was 9:04 A.M. The train was on time. I could see it through the glass windows at the top of the staircase. I bounded upward in singular leaps. The train was starting to move. I raced alongside and grasped a handrail with my free hand, barely pulling myself up onto the platform of the coach car. The train conductor at the top of the steps to the platform, a fatherly type, observing such daredevil tactics with disdain, looked at me disapprovingly and remarked, "It would be nice if you zipped your fly before you walk inside."

I walked directly to the club car and, between sips from a bottle of Budweiser, devoured all the information I possibly could absorb in my final review of the latest medical journals, which I had wisely taken with me.

At 2 P.M. the next day, in a state of euphoria, knowing I had performed perfectly in the exams, I ate lunch in the Wrigley Building with Judson Spencer, a college classmate, and treated myself to a martini. I boarded the sleeper for Hartford and remained undisturbed by the telephone for ten straight hours.

I was privileged to deliver Ethel three more times in subsequent years but without any semblance of the drama that accompanied the first occasion. In the total history of my service to Jack's family, including Ethel, his sister, and two sisters-in-law, I chalked up nine deliveries and four major operations.

And just to think, it all began with a salami sandwich in the fifth grade.

Chapter 10
Mud

"A straight line tracing from your fetal monitor is the most ominous sign of fetal distress. No beat-to-beat variability. Act at once." Dr. Schifrin and his fellow maternal/fetal experts echoed this somber dictum on all three days of the conference. Even if we forgot everything else presented to us in this national perinatology course, this admonition would most certainly be imprinted indelibly in our memories.

Rosalie O'Brien was the daughter of Joe Shea, a fellow coach with me in the West Hartford Boys Football League. He had advised Rosalie to use me as an obstetrician because he had deduced, most illogically, that since I seemed to be such a nice guy with the kids, I also must be a good doctor. Joe had registered a degree of concern because three years of marriage had passed without any attempt at contraception before pregnancy occurred. I promised him I would take good care of his daughter.

By 1970, fetal heart monitoring had become *de rigueur* on every hospital labor floor in America. My two younger partners were already mavens and I felt reasonably confident in interpreting the tracings. Yet, to feel as comfortable as possible and to give my patients the greatest benefit in this still new modality, I decided I needed some direct formal training. So I enrolled and participated in a national-level perinatology course in San Francisco directed by Barry S. Schifrin, M.D., considered at that time to be the leading authority in fetal heart rate monitoring in the country. The course ended at noon on Saturday and I flew back at once to Hartford to take over coverage of our practice early the next morning from one of my partners.

At 5:30 A.M., Sunday, I responded to Rosalie's call to the answering service and sent her in to Hartford Hospital in labor. She was at term in a very smooth and uneventful pregnancy.

Rosalie, her anxious husband and I arrived at the hospital simultaneously. Little did I know how fortuitous it was that I did not take my time, waiting at home for word from L and D as to the status of the labor. After all, I had given my promise to a special friend and I would have to be going in anyway to make rounds on other patients.

Rosalie was admitted and her labor was assessed as strong. The fetoscope to her abdomen revealed a regular fetal heart rate but it was slow at 100, the first sign off the norm. I quickly performed the vaginal exam and found the vertex (baby's head) well engaged with the cervix dilated at 3 cm. I artificially ruptured the membranes (bag of waters) and there emerged not the usual basically clear waters but a thick meconium-laced fluid substance that resembled mud—very frightening, the second warning. Just moments later the fetal monitor was attached revealing essentially a straight line with at best only a remote semblance of a beat. Certainly there was no real evidence of beat-to-beat change. I could feel Schifrin banging on my brain.

You could have heard me hollering downtown! "Stat section! Anesthesia! Neonatology!" All movement was lightning-fast. The anesthesiologists were magical in their speed. I dropped my street clothes right there on the floor. There was no time to change or to scrub. Clad only in my underwear, I was gowned and gloved in sterile gear and wielding the cesarean section scalpel faster than I deemed possible. Seconds later, or so it seemed, I pulled a gasping infant struggling for air through the uterine incision and handed it to the neonatologists, who were ready for action.

Intensive suction, expertly administered, was vital to clear the almost solid meconium from the pharynx and trachea of the newborn to create effective access for oxygen into the delicate new lungs. While closing, I watched intermittently as the neonatologists applied all their skills to bring that baby around. Those were memorably anxious moments indeed.

So what was the cause for all this grief? Once we could look inside, it was quite obvious: the umbilical cord was only five inches long, coming off a placenta attached to the fundus (top) of the uterus. The descent of the fetus during labor had produced an intolerable tension on the cord that certainly would have led to an intra-uterine fetal death in another few minutes.

The tension in the room was steadily diminishing. This new little girl was destined to be a fighter. At five minutes from birth, she was crying lustily and acting like any normal newborn of that age.

She made my day. In a little while I put my pants back on and made rounds. The San Francisco conference had paid an instant dividend.

Chapter 11
Police Call

"Dr. Grody, I'm in a room with a dead man." The words tumbled out of the telephone from a panic-stricken voice. It was 4 A.M.

As an obstetrician, I was accustomed to having the phone wake me at that hour to announce the onset of labor. A call bringing a message from the opposite end of life's spectrum was certainly the last thing I expected.

"I didn't know who else to call," Dorothy Reardon blurted as she identified herself. My wife, Sue, awakened by the ringing telephone, was at full alert from Dorothy's startling pronouncement, which she could clearly hear through the dead silence of the night. Usually, Sue was back in slumber before I finished conversing with patients who called at night. Not this time!

How was it that a patient could reach me directly without going through my answering service? It was my practice to give patients my home telephone number. That way, they could reach me directly in cases of emergency or extreme sensitivity in which they felt it necessary to bypass the answering service. For the most part, patients respected the privilege of possessing my home number and few abused it. In this particular case, both the emergency and sensitivity were obvious.

Dorothy, a delightful divorcee, and her three lovely daughters had been coming to the office for years for deliveries, surgery, and checkups. The office staff loved and always welcomed them.

"Dorothy," I asked, "Are you absolutely certain that he's dead?"

"Yes, his body went limp some time ago. He stopped breathing and there hasn't been any heart beat."

"Is he married?"

"Yes."

"Where is she?"

"In Florida."

"All right. Now listen closely and do exactly as I tell you. Dress him."

Startled, she answered, "Dress him?"

I replied, sternly, "Would you like him to be found in the nude? Hopefully, he's not too heavy for you. You must somehow get him into a chair."

"I'm strong enough. I can do that."

"Next, put a half-filled glass next to him. I'll bet there's one in the room. Are you with me?"

"Yes, I'm taking it all in," she responded.

"Then it will be time for you to dress and call the police. After you call, pull up a chair opposite his and have your drink handy."

Both curious and apprehensive, Dorothy asked, "What will I tell them?"

"It's obvious. The two of you were chatting over a late nightcap and he suddenly slumped down and stopped breathing."

"They'll never believe me!" she shrieked.

"Of course they won't believe you, but they will not question you either. They will nod and take notes. Count on it. They have real crimes to deal with."

"How do you know this?"

"Does either of you have a criminal record? Of course not. Just be sure to dress before you call the police. If they aren't busy, they can be there right away at this time of night. Oh, I almost forgot—after the police leave, call your lawyer. After, not before, because the lawyer could screw it all up. Besides, he'll charge you. I won't."

"I'll do as you say but I certainly am scared."

"Don't worry. You'll be okay. It's his wife who has the problem now, unfortunately. Be sure to call this afternoon to tell me how things worked out."

Dorothy did call later that day. She was greatly relieved and full of gratitude. The police had come, finished and departed in record time, all without incident.

Case closed.

Chapter 12
Tumor with a Heartbeat

"Terry, I'm sending over a 47-year-old lady with a growing pelvic tumor that's a little worrisome. It's producing some unusual G.I. symptoms," voiced my internist colleague, Dr. Seymour Solfeld, over the telephone.

Luckily a cancellation opened a space in an otherwise busy schedule for my office team to squeeze in Rhoda Rice. From the sound of it, immediate assessment seemed mandatory.

Mrs. Rice, appearing slightly apprehensive, came in with her husband, who was decidedly more anxious than his wife. I wasted no time in working up the case. The patient stated that she had entered menopause about five months previously. She said she realized that this was somewhat earlier than the average age for "the change of life" to begin but it followed the pattern set by her mother whose menses ceased at the same age. What she did not tell me was her mother's earlier history of two ovarian operations that involved significant reduction of ovarian tissue and which could have induced her early menopause. This I learned somewhat later when it didn't matter, but for the moment, lack of that knowledge threw my thinking off track.

Rhoda's gynecological history was notable only for absence of pregnancy despite no attempt at contraception during 22 years of a sexually active marriage. Recent digestive tract symptoms of nausea and indigestion had developed in association with increased girth of the lower abdomen. In the past two weeks there seemed to be marked overt "intestinal activity."

Physical examination revealed a healthy female with two unusual features. The breast bore some of the signs usually observed with pregnancy and a soft uterus was regularly enlarged to about the size of an 18 week intrauterine pregnancy.

Suddenly all the lights went on. The puzzle was solved. The last menstrual period was 20 weeks ago and there followed first trimester nausea. The recently observed increased "intestinal activity" was fetal movement. I broke out into a big grin as I reached for the fetoscope and placed the auditory cup against the lower abdomen. A crystal clear fetal heartbeat reached my eager ears as I listened while watching a bewildered husband wrenching his hands together. Without saying a word, I then applied the fetoscope to his ears and bade him to listen. Wide-eyed, he heard the joyful sounds as I gave the patient, ignored up to this point, a playful hug and welcomed her into the realm of motherhood.

The embrace of husband and wife that followed had to be as pure an expression of love and devotion as this earth has ever witnessed. It was such moments that reminded me how fortunate I was to be an obstetrician/gynecologist. With my eyes running tears, I left them alone to enjoy the surprise of their lifetime.

Then it was back to the real world. Foremost on the agenda was disclosure of the markedly significant increased incidence of mongolian trisomy defects in children born to women over 40. Would they want any testing to that effect to be done? Charles Rice's response was immediate and definitive. "If the good Lord meant this to happen, then that's how we'll take it. Besides, he did the same for Sarah, who was certainly no spring chicken when she presented Abraham with Isaac, and they seemed to do okay."

Rhoda then remained on an idyllic path for the balance of her gestation. She was a delightful patient who always brought good cheer into the office on her visits. Her husband, who took off from his business to accompany her, was equally beloved by the office staff with his joking attitude. They made the practice of medicine seem more like fun than work.

Exactly on her due date Rhoda delivered a healthy normal boy. Mr. Rice was enraptured and claimed he was still in a state of disbelief. Our office, happy for Rhoda, rued the end of her visits.

As for Dr. Solfeld, the referring physician, he wondered if he shouldn't have a fetoscope available to listen to any future intra-abdominal tumors he might encounter.

It took several days before we finished off the ten-pound box of chocolates Charles dropped off at the office.

Chapter 13
Marbles

"Dr. Grody, I've been feeling marbles in my belly since this morning and maybe they're getting worse," came Nancy's frantic cry over the telephone late one afternoon.

"How do you feel otherwise?" I asked.

"I feel just great."

She then answered in the negative to all the standard questions, i.e., fever, nausea, loss of appetite, fatigue, diarrhea, and constipation, but she did say that she had "been very careless with" her diet the past few days.

Nancy was a very loyal and beloved patient of several years whom I had delivered twice. A simple soul of no intellectual depth, she was prone to unusual imaginative complaints that had never yet amounted to anything of consequence.

"My dear, it's probably only gas and nothing to worry about, but if you still have those marbles tomorrow morning, call and come in so I can check you."

Seemingly reassured, she hung up. However, she was on the phone again at 8:30 A.M. the next morning to announce the continued presence of the marbles. So we squeezed her into the schedule and brought her into an examining room at 11:45 A.M.

"Nancy, I'm checking your abdomen carefully and deeply and I simply cannot find any marbles. Show me."

With a quizzical look on her face, she reached down, felt around, and exclaimed, "My Lord, they're all gone!"

"Between the time you called this morning and now, did you have one hell of a big bowel movement?"

"Yes, I did! It doubled me over."

With a very serious mien, I then pronounced, "Nancy, I think you have lost your marbles."

With this, Barbara, the nurse in attendance, could not contain herself and burst out in laughter while I broke out into a big grin.

"You're laughing at me!"

"Hardly. Look at yourself—even you are all smiles at the joke. We are laughing *with* you, not at you. I couldn't pass it up. Besides, isn't it great that you have nothing to worry about and to know that we would never let you down? We will always be there for you. There is no charge for the visit. Now go home and enjoy your day."

She gave me a big hug and left. She continued as a loyal patient. We never did let her down.

Chapter 14
Trash Can Caper

"Okay, here's the second graft, let's wrap it with the first one in a moist (cotton) sponge while we close the graft sites," I said as I moved the segment of harvested skin over to the instrument table. Six people were scrubbed, including two nurses who, most of all, should have been able to put their hands directly on the first graft. It was gone. They had no idea what had happened to it. Neither did the other three scrubbed doctors or any of the 12 doctors, there to observe this unusual operation, or additional nurses in the room. The missing graft was not to be found anywhere on the entire sterile operative surfaces.

I was furious. I cut loose with raw invective. As we were preparing for the surgery some 90 minutes earlier, I had taken great pains to warn everyone in the room against letting this happen, not to discard mistakenly any moist sponge that might have a graft wrapped inside. Nobody had been listening, apparently. Everybody must have thought I was talking to someone else.

In 1993, I had devised my own modified operative technique for restoring a functional vagina when the original vagina had literally disappeared secondary either to overzealous original vaginal surgery and/or recurrent surgery and/or over-reactive scarring response to corrective pelvic surgery. The usual result, after such mayhem, is bladder and rectum, with no intervening vagina, bound against each other by tough scar tissue, outside of which is usually found a residual vaginal dimple of one to three centimeters in depth. The very challenging vaginal restitution procedure is accomplished by skillfully combining direct pelvic maneuvers and intra-abdominal laparoscopic guidance. Then, two full-thickness skin grafts, one from each flank, are harvested, carefully stripped clean of all extraneous tissue, and sutured together to form a sac which, when slipped in between the previously separated bladder and rectum, adopts the role of a functional neovagina.

I had gained a reputation as an expert in this sophisticated type of surgery from conference exposure of a video I had produced of it. This film was initially shown at the annual meeting of the American College of Obstetricians and Gynecologists in San Francisco in April, 1995, and later at the annual meeting of the Society of Gynecologic Surgeons in New Orleans in March, 1996. Thereafter, it was shown at a number of clinical conferences and continues to be shown to this day.

As a consequence of the publicity the video received, the U.S. Government had invited me to be a guest professor for one week at the largest U.S. military hospital serving full families of military and government personnel. The GYN service there had lined up several difficult cases for me to perform with them for educational purposes. One of the cases was a post-surgical obliterated vagina that they had saved for me to work on so they could observe live what they already had seen in my video.

So here we were, stymied, after meticulously bringing the operation to its climactic point, for lack of one-half of a new vagina. After several moments of fruitless search on both tables and in the folds of the enveloping operating sheets, I let out a commanding, "Stop!" Everyone stood still.

"Look inside that trash can adjacent to the far operating table where we keep the sponges for a count at the end of the operation. Open each sponge carefully without touching the inner surface. Inside one, carefully wrapped, you are going to find our missing graft."

And so we did, to the embarrassment of all. With close attention, we washed the graft copiously with saline and antibiotic solutions. The operation was then completed to precise satisfaction. The post-operative course and specific care all went smooth as silk both before and after my return to Philadelphia.

I remained in close telephone contact with my military colleagues to follow the patient's progress for many weeks. At six months I was informed that she had fully healed and was functioning sexually like any other female.

Now just how often does one come across a story in which half a vagina has taken a trip through a trash can?

Chapter 15
Three Loops

"Let's move! Open the section room. Have anesthesia take over the epidural stat. I want a high enough level." I could not wait another second; the stakes were too high. Hopefully we hadn't blown it already.

Louise was 40 years old. Fourteen years earlier, she had married Herb Rheinhard, a dear high school classmate of mine. Five years ago, quite some time after they had given up on bearing their own children, secondary to oligospermia, she began coming to my office for regular annual checkups. They finally decided to seek adoption. I was helping them in the process. Nine months previously, the adoption procedure was nearing completion. Soon thereafter, Louise missed her period. Herb was ecstatic!

Early that morning, Louise had completed a totally uneventful and normal pregnancy by going into labor exactly on her due date. I sent her down to Hartford Hospital where she was admitted and attached to a fetal monitor as she made initial progress.

I began my morning office hours, only ten minutes away from the hospital, with intermittent telephone calls to the labor and delivery floor to keep track of progress. At 10:40 A.M., I was informed that the vertex was well engaged at station 0. The cervix was dilated to 4 centimeters and the bag of waters had ruptured. I ordered epidural analgesia to be started. All was going well.

At 12:05 P.M., the start of lunch break, I drove down to the hospital to check Louise myself and to reassure both Louise and Herb that everything was progressing favorably.

The examination itself was reassuringly positive. The cervix was almost completely dilated and the vertex was approaching the pelvic floor. The labor was strong, the fetal heart rate (FHR) was steady at a normal 130, and delivery was probably just one hour away.

Suddenly, as we sat there waiting and chatting, changes occurred that made me jump. The FHR dropped to 105-110, the fetal heart monitor tracing began showing some late decelerations, and meconium (fetal stool) began to appear from the vagina. Any one of these changes in isolation might raise only slight suspicion of potential problems but, with all appearing together, especially in a case like this, unease was hardly the term to describe our emotions.

Immediately, all the standard palliative measures, including change of position and oxygen, were brought into play. We were reasonably sure that the umbilical cord had not slipped into a compromising position. With delivery time imminent and taking into account my skill with forceps, it was not unreasonable to continue plans for a vaginal delivery. After five minutes of effort and intense observation, however, reversion to normal seemed insufficient.

I had had enough. Adoption had been discarded. It was possible now that we could lose this baby. The final score could be zero and I would never forgive myself for the rest of my life.

My hands were flying. Eleven minutes after I had ordered a

cesarean section, I was pulling a healthy normal 7 pound 11 ounce male infant through a standard low transverse uterine incision. My own heart rate returned to normal levels. Herb, an effusive new daddy, who had been present throughout the proceedings and photographing uninterruptedly, almost contaminated the operative field with his emotional display of gratitude. Then he nearly dropped his camera as he wrapped loving arms around Hartford Hospital's latest admission. When we asked Herb how he had remained in such fine control up to the actual delivery while the rest of us were on pins and needles, he said that he just had a feeling of complete confidence.

So what could have caused the adverse changes that forced my decision to deliver by section? The umbilical cord was strung in three loops around the infant's neck. The tension thereby created with each uterine contraction, although not life-threatening over the short term, was enough to render undesirable signs and an obstetrician's fits.

In review, could I have waited a little longer and performed this delivery safely per vagina? Objectively, most likely, yes. Realistically, all things considered, I had made the only rational choice. Gambling was not appropriate. Success was proclaimed in the baby's cry.

Slightly late, I returned to my office—now crammed with patients—with a light heart. My good deed for the day had been done.

Chapter 16
Mum's the Word

"How's your mum?" she asked, in her patent British accent as we chatted in my office after her annual physical exam. She seemed quite remorseful as she asked this question.

Mrs. Myra Hodges had been a regular patient dating back eleven years, about six years after her post-World War II arrival in the U.S. as a war bride. She was eternally grateful for the hysterectomy I had performed to remove a very early uterine cervical cancer. Periodically she would bring in a token gift at her visits, like a small cake or some dark chocolates, to which I have an addiction.

"How in blazes does she know my mother?" I silently asked myself. Anyway, I figured that I certainly didn't know everything that was going on. Perhaps they had met at a bridge tournament or a mah-jongg party. Whatever, I may have forgotten something and there may have been a relationship that I had tuned out for some reason.

Nonetheless, not wanting to act like a boob, I took a shot in the dark and answered, with full courtesy, "Just fine, how's yours?"

"Dead," came the sorrowful response.

"How terrible!" I countered. Well, when a physician's sympathy is called for, there are few who can compete with me. After I felt I had carried on sufficiently, professional curiosity prompted the usual query as to the cause of death.

"You know those trucks that come around in the winter and spray out all that heavy salt to melt the ice? Well, the weather was so bad this year they overdid it and knocked out all my beds."

Suddenly the light came on. She was talking about chrysanthemums, with no parental reference intended. I had forgotten that she was a chrysanthemum expert and had presented me with one of her prize plants at her last visit.

I couldn't wait for her to leave the office before racing to share the hysterical story, between guffaws, with the office staff.

Needless to say, my "mum" was thriving in the sunshine on our patio!

Chapter 17
Night Call

The last thing I needed that night was any unnecessary or undesirable disturbance, like fire truck sirens or barking dogs or thunderclaps. For two straight nights I had been up at all hours with deliveries. I needed a break, desperately.

It was not to be.

"Dr. Grody, it's Gloria Stoughton from Middletown calling. How are you?" sang the chirpy notes from the telephone.

Middletown is about 18 minutes due south of Hartford and, at the time, was home to, among other things, the state psychiatric hospital. Gloria was an exacting and exhausting patient, relentless in her pursuit of senseless ideas, the kind of woman I wished had chosen another doctor. She had an infertility problem.

"How am I?" I was not pleased. "You don't want to know," I spoke into the phone.

Despite the overwhelming courtesy of the vast majority of my patients over the years, there were a few who seemed to believe that inherent somewhere in the Hippocratic Oath was the phrase "I am now a doctor, so it's okay to bother me any time you wish."

"Gloria," I asked, "What time do you have there in Middletown right now?"

"Why, it's 2:10 A.M.

"Funny thing—that's exactly the same time we have here in West Hartford."

I could see that Sue, too, was now unwillingly wide awake.

Ignoring my comment and rolling merrily along, behaving as though this were a routine situation, Gloria continued, "Greg and I have been discussing our case and all the possibilities you explained to us."

We had run Gloria and her husband through a full gamut of tests and had concluded that any potential for success in solving their infertility resided in what we might accomplish via laparoscopy and possibly laparotomy. I had explained the details to them. She was now begging the question and waiting for a comment from me, so I said, questioningly, "Yes?"

"I want to go ahead with the operation."

"Fine," I replied. I continued, "Tomorrow morning, when regular hospital business resumes, we will call Hartford Hospital and schedule you for admission and surgery. Then I will phone you at this same time tomorrow to give you the date."

"Are you crazy?" shrieked my beloved patient at the other end of the line.

I retorted, "Somehow I got the impression that that was the appropriate hour to conduct business in Middletown."

We concluded the conversation and hung up. Sue and I looked at each other and broke out laughing. "Did this really happen?" she asked.

I made all the arrangements and the operation achieved the intended goal. Three months later Gloria conceived and then enjoyed what was a normal pregnancy for her and a fittingly nightmarish ordeal for me. Three years later she was rewarded with another healthy infant and I with nine more months of suffering.

Hippocrates would have been pleased.

Chapter 18
Lettuce

"Something terrible has happened to me. Please fit me in sometime today," came the plaintive tones at 9 o'clock on a Monday morning.

Maria Della Rossi, a flaky but endearing woman, was one of my earliest patients. I had delivered her last baby during my second year of practice. Now, ten years later, at 45 years of age, she had become a "regular" for scheduled annual exams. We had become accustomed to her occasionally peculiar medical complaints, never serious, born of a vivid imagination. I thought I had heard just about everything but today, courtesy of Maria, I would be told a story that was beyond fiction.

Of course we would see her. My staff knew my rule: When patients called in a state of urgency, we would always find a way to work them in.

Maria fluttered into an examining room and could hardly wait for the attendant to come through the door.

"It was just awful," she burst out as she thrust herself without delay on the table and into a pelvic exam position. "Last evening I was in my cousin's kitchen helping set up for her daughter's engagement party. I was sitting on a high stool next to the counter, preparing food, when her cat raced across the room and jumped up and bit me in my lettuce."

Luckily I was able to pull the examining sheet up in front of me as I sat down and began to crack up while Jane, our aide, entered the room. This was a new one for me. I could barely hold back my laughter. Sitting at the foot of the table and hiding below the level of the exam sheet covering the lower half of the patient's body, while Jane looked on curiously, I asked Maria if she would not mind repeating the story so I could be sure I had it straight.

And so she did, ending again with "the cat jumped up and bit me in my lettuce." Hearing a very muffled chuckle from me, she added, "Isn't that what they call it?" with which I retorted, as I conducted the pelvic exam, "It all depends on how you take your salad." On this note, while tears were rolling down my cheeks, Jane hastily begged leave of the room for a moment as she bit her lower lip in emotional restraint.

My exam uncovered no lesions, only healthy external genitalia and, as Jane was returning into the room, she heard me tell Maria, "You don't have to worry. Your lettuce is fine and needs no dressing."

As Jane assisted the patient off the table, I advised her that, if she ever again planned a similar culinary adventure in her cousin's kitchen, she should precede it by a visit to Modell's Sport Center to purchase a male athletic cup for protection. I thought Jane was going to slug me.

I closed the visit with "There's no charge for today. Enjoy the engagement party."

So ended a memorable day in the expansion of the descriptive landscape of the female genital tract.

Chapter 19
On Edge

Blood burst out in a river! It was as though the left lateral end of the uterine incision had exploded.

Joy Wilkins was at term and in labor at Hartford Hospital in the wee hours of the night in October 1970. I had come down to the hospital at about 10 P.M. to be with her until delivery, which I estimated would happen about 1 to 2 A.M. at the rate she was going. It was now 4 A.M. and she was making no further progress. The cervix had been fully dilated for 90 minutes and the vertex had been stuck one centimeter below the ischial spine for one hour, despite strong labor. The fetal monitor indicated that the baby was in good shape.

Despite the patient's fervent wish to be allowed to deliver naturally, it was time for cesarean section. This was a cut and dried situation of true cephalo-pelvic disproportion, i.e., the baby's head simply was not going to fit through 5'2" Joy's pelvis despite what had been thought to be adequate measurements. This infant, as we later observed after delivery, had a large cranium and weighed 9 lbs 2 oz—just too much baby for this mother.

We set about preparing for the delivery by section anticipating no unusual problems. The standard approach was made with the usual low transverse uterine incision. The infant's head was relatively large and so well entrenched in the pelvis that we found it necessary to employ the cesarean forceps to ease the head gently through the uterine incision.

My patient extracting efforts were to no avail. The left end of the uterine incision tore apart like putty and extended downward and posteriorly toward the cul-de-sac. Blood was streaming from the newly torn edges secondary to the proximity of left uterine vessels. In a split second, I flipped the uterus out onto the abdominal wall and, with hands flying, I threw in a continuous locking suture with record speed. The bleeding was thwarted almost as quickly as it had begun. Smiles all around; we were in and out of trouble quickly and had responded just as we were supposed to in sudden emergency situations.

The first uterine incision closure layer having thus been started in the torn extension, the balance of it was then completed with the same suture length. The second outer closure layer was placed in routine fashion.

In several respects, this caesarean section had not followed the normal path. Under normal circumstances, clamps are quickly placed on large bleeders followed by tying or suturing. In this case, massive bites with the clamps would have been needed. That would have coincidentally crushed and destroyed a significant amount of uterine tissue, which would have led to a weaker scar than would result if clamping were avoided. The weak scar would have increased the risk of uterine rupture in the next pregnancy. Our direct suture approach was used to circumvent such a defect.

Also, it was not my usual practice in cesarean sections to lift the uterus out of the pelvis and onto the abdominal wall to close the uterine incision, followed by replacement of the uterus inside the abdomen upon completion. My view was that this commonly used technique certainly made the physician's job easier but it also tended to place undue and unnecessary strain on uterine blood vessels and supports. It was not really that much more difficult, and clearly better for the patient, to close the incision, employing appropriate maneuvers, with the uterus in situ. In this unusual case, however, with the markedly extended tear posteriorly and downward, complicated by hemorrhage, it became imperative to create operative accessibility by lifting the uterus outside the abdominal cavity.

With a healthy newborn asserting his presence intermittently in a crib in the background, we thought we were on the road home. Replace the uterus into the pelvis, sew the abdomen closed, and catch another hour of sleep before the regular day's activities would begin.

I grasped the uterus firmly and pressed it into the abdominal opening. It would not budge. I shifted it this way and I shifted it that way. Nothing worked. It simply would not slide back into the patient's body. Was I dreaming? A uterus that would not go back inside through an incision that was large enough for it to be brought outside? I had never heard of such a thing. I began to feel very stupid until my hands, investigating circumferentially, uncovered the problem. Hidden behind the uterus, about four centimeters of the upper edge of the transverse abdominal skin incision had, in the haste of placing the life-saving continuous stitch in the sea of gushing blood, been trapped in its first five uterine closure loops. There could, of course, be no release of the uterus.

"Oh, no," groaned the chief resident, scrubbed opposite me. "We're going to have to take down the entire closure and, bleeding and all, do it all over again."

"Like hell," I retorted. "You and I are about to do something we've never heard of before." As everyone watched, with a scalpel I stripped a quarter-inch-by-four-centimeters length of involved skin edge from its abdominal wall attachment without disturbing one iota any of the stitches placed in the uterus. Now free, the uterus slipped gently back into its normal position with no fuss. We closed the abdomen in standard fashion. The left abdominal incision end was adjusted cosmetically so that the small strip of skin, now in its new home, would never be missed.

Grinning widely, I proclaimed, "You are all staring at the only woman on this planet who treasures a small segment of abdominal skin in the area of her cul-de-sac."

We all caught that last hour of sleep. Both the patient and her new infant enjoyed uneventful hospital courses.

Two years later, at a repeat section of a slightly smaller baby, there were no dramatic surprises. I could hardly wait, once we had lifted the infant out, to inspect the cul-de-sac. I found it to be in pristine condition. There was no visible evidence that anything unusual had ever happened there.

How about that for a storybook ending?

Chapter 20
Tragedy of the Worst Kind

She would never reach her 22nd birthday, and it all had begun so joyously as she turned 20, one year after she had married.

During the 32 years I worked in Hartford, I practiced obstetrics as well as general gynecology. Over the course of some 5,500 deliveries during that period, I encountered two deaths among my own patients. They were horrible experiences that cracked so indelibly into my psyche that I live with their memories perhaps more deeply than all other events of my life. In neither case was I the cause of or a contributor to the demise of the patient but the two tragic events did occur while the patients were in my care.

Marcia Rothberg was a bubbly bright young woman who was first seen in the third month of her first pregnancy. Her mother, a longtime, faithful and beloved gynecologic patient, had referred her. I had promised the mother that I would give her daughter good care.

The pregnancy appeared to be normal for a healthy young patient in all respects, including the full physical exam. However, at about the 19th week of gestation Marcia noted an area of her breast that was growing inordinately. Immediate investigation was mandatory. We discovered a distinct lump of firm consistency that could not be considered a normal response to pregnancy. Biopsy revealed a singularly aggressive cancer, to my profound astonishment. This was the ultimate "unthinkable" in one so young. I was mortified. I just could not believe that such a thing was happening, but it was starkly real.

The balance of Marcia's short life was consumed with surgery, irradiation, chemotherapy, multiple fruitless consultations, and secondary intrauterine fetal death at 28 weeks. No words can describe the relentless and merciless pain and despair endured by the patient so afflicted, not to mention the torture the family of one so young was forced to experience. Marcia died 18 months after the bleak diagnosis.

What about the physician? "It goes with the territory." "Get over it and go on with your practice. These things happen, sooner or later, to all of us." "You didn't cause the cancer—you just got stuck with it." One platitude after another was available for refuge but my devastation was unrelieved. Was I able to continue to do my job effectively? For week after week, in the aftermath, I awakened and went to bed with dreadful thoughts of this case. The despair of losing a patient does not ever go away.

Chapter 21
Inside Out

"Before you leave, Dr. Grody, please take a look into D.R.3. The residents are having a terrible problem with bleeding in a patient they just delivered." So was I addressed by the head nurse one afternoon in January 1981.

I had just performed a routine vaginal delivery on one of my own private patients in Delivery Room 5. On the way to the locker room so I could dress back into my street clothes and return to my office, I noticed a commotion in D.R.3. When I paused to size up the situation, it appeared to be under control, so I continued on to doff my scrub suit and prepare to leave.

I changed rapidly. I knew patients were piled up waiting to be seen and I wanted to get back to them. I rushed to the elevator.

That's when the head nurse intercepted and redirected me. There was indeed trouble in D.R.3. In no small measure, blood was dripping onto the floor at the foot of the delivery table.

"What's going on?" I cried.

The chief resident answered in anxious tones, "We're trying to replace a large intrauterine fibroid that popped out immediately after we delivered the placenta."

That certainly sounded peculiar. "There must have been some suspicion of this in her prenatal records. What is recorded?" I asked.

"This is really all a complete surprise," came the response.

It was time for swift action. I jumped into the room, street clothes and all. A hand on the abdomen suprapubically showed no evidence of any immediate post-partum uterus, which should have been easily palpable. As I tore off my suit jacket, I barked out to the anesthesiologist, "Put her down deep, as fast as you can." We had an inverted uterus on our hands, a very serious complication of delivery if not addressed immediately.

I slipped into sterile gloves in split seconds and shortly my hands were firmly grasping the uterus, turned inside out and hanging over the edge of the table. The anesthesiologist reacted promptly and efficiently while announcing that the patient was about to go into shock. Then, with all my might, with the full thrust of my body weight and as a junior resident on each side held the patient in fixed position, I forced the uterus into reversion and back into the pelvis, not a moment too soon. Seconds more and the uterus would have been incarcerated outside the body with the need for emergency hysterectomy in a life-saving situation.

We were not yet out of the woods. The bleeding, although considerably reduced now, continued. I called for intravenous Methergine in maximum dosage to maintain the uterus in a contracted state while my left hand forcefully held it in elevation and the anesthesiologist fed 100% oxygen into the patient's lungs. Fortunately, the residents had prepared for potential blood replacement so we were now able to push blood into her circulation and pull her out of shock.

It was a very humble and somewhat ashamed group of resident physicians that finished work that day. It is reasonable to assume that they would never forget the experience and would be better practitioners as a result of it.

Needless to say, my shirt and tie were ruined and enough blood had settled on my trousers to create quite an unacceptable appearance. So, once I was certain that all was in control in the delivery room, I changed back into a scrub suit and conducted the balance of my office hours in that attire.

By sheer coincidence, as I began to record my personal experience with this very uncommon complication of delivery, a case report on such a situation appeared in the February 2006 issue of the journal "Contemporary OB/GYN." In that instance, delay in recognition of and response to the dire situation resulted in hysterectomy. Unquestionably, the occurrence of uterine inversion coincides with expulsion of the placenta. My considered opinion, although not yet validated by any empirical research of which I am aware, is that the great majority, if not all, of the cases result from overeagerness that leads to yanking on the umbilical cord that turns the uterus inside out.

Chapter 22
The Newborn Cried as Its Mother Died

"Terry, the patient stopped breathing. She's dead," declared Dr. Bobrow, the anesthesiologist, aghast, at the head of the table.

Simultaneously, out popped a healthy nine-pound female with a cry that its mother would never hear.

Air embolism is a rare cause of maternal death, rare enough that the odds were against its occurrence at any time in my practice. Yet here it happened, in stark reality; unpredictable, unpreventable, irremediable.

An embolism is any substance not normally found in the blood circulation that enters it and is moved within it. The most common form is a thrombus, a clot that forms inside a vein that, when loosened, is propelled through the venous circulation to the lungs, where it can be, and often is, immediately lethal. A similarly deadly situation can occur at delivery if a large pocket of air is sucked into an open uterine vein at the site of placental separation. This rare phenomenon happens when the newborn is delivered rather explosively with simultaneous separation of the placenta. Such a situation can set up negative pressure in the uterus so that air is literally sucked into large exposed venous openings in deadly fashion. That is precisely what happened with 28-year-old Mary McIntyre. She gave one huge push in association with a strong uterine contraction, delivered a healthy infant and placenta simultaneously, and died. I never, before or since that moment, felt so utterly and devastatingly helpless.

Autopsy verified the diagnosis of air embolus.

A mother's death at the moment of her child's birth is perhaps the most horrible medical irony. There is no way for the physician to escape the family's agony from such an awful and heartbreaking experience. It was the lowest point of my career. I went to the funeral. I cried with the family. I mourned with the family. I live forever with the memory of that horrible episode.

Chapter 23

Good Deed from a Bread Knife on Good Friday

"Come quickly, Dr. Grody! A patient just died out on the floor," they cried as they yanked on my arm. What a way to be pulled from a doze induced by a very technical medical article.

Four-bed wards were hospital standards for clinic post-partum patients in 1959 and it was routine to place undelivered patients who required hospital observation in proximity to post-partum patients. Mrs. Celia Brown, someone unknown to me, was a 42-year-old very recent widow in her 39th week of pregnancy. Bearing a history of angina pectoris and with recent development of hypertension, she had been hospitalized one week earlier for bed rest with bathroom privileges only, to be observed while awaiting the onset of labor.

It was visiting hours, usually the quietest and most serene daylight period in a hospital, especially in a post-partum unit where happiness over new babies permeates the atmosphere. And this particular day was Good Friday, one that had promised to be especially quiet and characteristically uneventful. Three of the nursing personnel I employed for many years were devout Catholics, so I always closed the office on Good Friday out of respect for them. That gave me an opportunity to induce labor in indicated cases and to read and write while monitoring the progress of the labors.

Suddenly, there were cries for my assistance. Springing from my chair, I raced after the distressed nurses down the hall to a four-bed enclosure jammed with visitors. Lying prostrate across the far left bed, surrounded by aghast relatives, lay the body of a woman I quickly assessed as dead—but not lifeless! The nurses screamed, "What about the baby?" The woman was still pregnant! No time for questions, I tore off to the kitchen, snatched up the bread knife lying fortuitously on the table, and seconds later, after two quick slashes through the abdomen and the uterus, pulled out a healthy baby with, amazingly, a spontaneous lusty cry.

Clasping the cut cord with my bare hand, I bounded into the nursery where, a few seconds later, the cord was clamped and a normal newborn infant was settled into a crib. Nearby, a female visitor at a neighboring bedside had fainted during the critical harrowing moments of the publicly exposed post-mortem cesarean section. I plopped into the nearest chair and took several deep breaths, overwhelmed by the spectacle in which I had just played a role on Good Friday, April 12, 1959.

The following Monday morning, Dr. Isadore Geetter, the President of Mount Sinai Hospital in Hartford, asked me into his office after I had completed rounds. He expressed overwhelming gratitude on behalf of the hospital for my action in saving the baby on Friday. In response, I told him that I happened to be the only obstetrician around at the time and simply performed the way any other doctor would have under the circumstances. Besides, I told him, it was really the nursing staff that deserved the congratulations. They had performed all the quick thinking and I had merely been the mechanic.

Dr. Geetter informed me that the autopsy on Mrs. Brown revealed death due to sudden massive heart attack. Her 23-year-old son and his wife had already initiated plans to adopt the baby.

Chapter 24
Leak

"You're just not going to believe this," announced Eileen, the private GYN clinic receptionist at Temple University Hospital. "There's a 98-year-old woman out there registering right now to see you."

"Oh, no," I groaned. What a way to start afternoon office hours. "Disabled and in a wheelchair, no doubt," anticipating the usual presentation for a patient in that age group.

"Not at all. That's the surprise," answered Eileen. "She walked in on her own steam, without any support. She says she's here to get surgery."

"You're kidding! Is she for real?"

"She's sharp as a razor, and her whole family is with her. There must be six of them."

I had operated on a number of women in their early 90's in the past but never on anyone this old. The usual procedure was for vaginal obliteration to overcome terrible disabilities arising from extreme prolapse in cases where pessaries were no longer a mechanical non-surgical option. The surgery for this closure was actually simple, lasting an average of only 40 minutes and requiring minimal anesthesia, and it afforded reasonable comfort for the few remaining years of life. That sort of situation was what I anticipated I was about to see. I was wrong. It was much more complicated.

Mary Shanahan was ushered into my consultation room with three doting children and three loving grandchildren. We squeezed four of them into seats. An amazing and utterly unique story then began to unfold.

Mary Shanahan was as delightful and charming a patient as I had ever encountered. Her rich brogue sounded as though it had arrived from Dublin the day before. She was as bright as a new penny and literally sparkled with personality and humor despite her age and the very debilitating condition that precipitated her visit to my office. Mrs. Shanahan's problem was a huge vesicovaginal fistula. This is a hole between the bladder and the vagina through which urine dribbles continuously. Such a fistula is usually the result of surgical injury or trauma from a vaginal delivery. Not so in this case where a very rare cause was to blame.

"I'm soaking wet 24 hours a day. I seem to be spending all my time changing from one Depends to another. My bottom and upper thighs are raw and irritated. This has been going on now for ten months. It's making my life miserable. I need this fixed." So declared this lovely lady.

Eighteen years earlier Mary had opted for correction of a massive uteropelvic prolapse by the placement of a very large stem pessary in her vagina rather than undergoing pelvic reconstructive surgery. A pessary is a device that elevates and holds the prolapsed pelvic organs back within the body. However, the patient is obligated to return to the gynecologist's office every 8-10 weeks so the pessary can be cleaned and checked for position, while the vagina is simultaneously examined to note whether or not there are any signs of erosion into the vaginal wall. In order to avoid problems, it is essential that these visits not be neglected. The patient is also required to inject a small amount of estrogen cream intravaginally 2-3 times per week. This helps to maintain a healthy vaginal wall of normal thickness and flexibility to protect the patient from the pressure applied by the pessary.

One of two paths with reference to pessary employment usually follows over time from one patient to another. Either the pessary works effectively until the patient's death, or, in other cases, the residual supportive tissues, still strong enough at the outset of pessary placement, gradually deteriorate to a point where the pessary will no longer hold its effective position. In the latter instance, relief can be obtained only through surgery, either pelvic reconstruction or vaginal obliteration.

Sometimes the pelvic tissues, with the pessary in position, can follow a reverse course, especially in the absence of estrogen cream application. In these situations, progressive dense fibrotic constriction narrows the vagina and the vaginal introitus. When that occurs, neglect of pessary maintenance care inevitably leads to erosion, either toward the bladder anteriorly, as in Mary's case, or toward the rectum posteriorly, due to progressive constrictive force.

A stem pessary, which was the type that the family said had been used in their mother, is shaped like a mushroom. The round flat table of this device is positioned in the patient to extend from the vaginal entry behind the urethra internally against the entire anterior vaginal wall, behind the cystocele (prolapsed bladder), to the area deep in the vagina behind the cervix. The width of the pessary locks it in place. The stem or knob of the device points backward and toward the lower rectum. It can be very effective in overcoming a prolapse, as it obviously was in this case.

Initially, Mary Shanahan had periodic regular examinations but then neglected to return because of the absence of any symptoms.

For whatever reason, she never used intravaginal estrogen cream and she had never been put on any hormone replacement regimen. After her incontinence began, numerous gynecologists and urologists had seen Mary. It was quite obvious that the pessary had eroded, under the pressure of constriction, into the bladder, thereby creating a fistula through which urine leaked into the vagina and then outside the body. All attempts to remove the pessary, both on an outpatient basis and under anesthesia, had been unsuccessful.

A son spoke up, saying, "The last doctor we saw told us that our only chance for getting help for our mother was with you."

Now there was a challenge I didn't ask for. I answered this comment at first with a blank stare and then the noncommittal words, "We shall see."

Examination revealed urine flowing from a markedly constricted vagina through a vaginal introitus that only admitted an index finger. The knob of the pessary was palpated with the fingertip. The pessary had eroded completely into the bladder through the anterior vaginal wall. Under such circumstances, positive maneuvers were impossible. Rectal exam disclosed a tiny post-menopausal uterus locked firmly in a well-elevated position. Otherwise this mentally lucid female was in excellent health.

Both oral and intravaginal estrogen therapy were initiated to restore tissue resiliency in preparation for surgery.

Six weeks later, under anesthesia, deep incisions were made on either side of the vagina to provide adequate access. Then with extreme difficulty and extensive manipulation, after hooking tenacula into the firm plastic pessary stem for traction and applying copious lubrication, the enormous mushroom top, measuring three inches in diameter and lying totally inside the bladder, was extracted. A huge commensurate linear hole (fistula) with swollen traumatized edges was apparent. The openings of the ureters from the kidneys were, fortunately, seen to be safely aside. The bilateral incisions were closed easily in standard fashion.

A thorough search of the medical literature yielded only three other cases of vesicovaginal fistula from a neglected pessary but nothing close to the magnitude of this case or to this patient's age.

At this point, I discussed with the patient and her family the further intricate surgery that would be necessary to attempt to close the huge fistulous opening and the attendant risks. Mary felt she had no choice and declared vehemently that she would rather die than continue living with this leaking disability. Then I explained that, although the only three other somewhat similar cases reported involved corrective operations through an abdominal approach, we would take the vaginal route. I would opt for this method, I told her, because even though the abdominal exposure allowed for a much less technically demanding effort than the precise skill required in her case for the closure procedure from below, the risks were far less for a woman of her age by the latter plan. Besides, I believed that with my experience in vaginal surgery, I probably could do the job faster that way.

Estrogen replacement was continued for the next nine weeks to further enhance tissue receptivity to surgery and to allow recovery from the damage inflicted at pessary retrieval. Then, after making the same two deep lateral incisions for operative access, appropriate perifistulous vaginal denudation was accomplished, followed by the required meticulous three-layer closure of the formidable large defect.

For the next six days, during which Mary Shanahan enjoyed a serene recovery, my colleagues and I held our collective breaths. Even under the best circumstances, vesicovaginal fistula closure procedures recorded a ten percent failure rate, which would become manifest within six days. The sun rose on the seventh morning and she remained dry as a bone. She voided urine only at will and continued to do so for the next four years.

This singular remarkably successful case was reported on pages 407-408 of the June 1999 issue of the International Urogynecological Journal.

Chapter 25
Upside Down

I thought that, in my vast experience and exposure during more than 50-odd years in gynecology, I had either seen or heard of every kind of oddball uterus shape or position that could possibly exist, but this one exceeded anything I could have even imagined. Thus it was, in the end, no real surprise that it led to one of my most unusual and challenging surgical adventures.

This uterine tale begins on November 5, 1996, when Rosemary Cartland, a healthy 38-year-old mother of three children, all delivered vaginally at full-term size, appeared in my Temple University office on referral from her internist for surgery. "Dr. Charles Shuman told me I would need a hysterectomy. I had heard that the uterus could be removed from the vagina, rather than the abdomen, but when I asked him if that could be done in my case, he said he didn't think so because my uterus was so large. Then he said that the only doctor he knew who could do it, if it was possible, would be you. That's why I'm here."

Rosemary's history was classic for the progressive development and growth of the commonly occurring "fibroid uterus." So-called fibroids are benign tumors consisting of combinations of fibrous tissue and muscle-resemblant tissue that are of no concern until they enlarge the uterus to the point of disabling symptoms. Rosemary's case was typical, with indigestion, increased abdominal girth, interference with bowel movements, urinary frequency, and pelvic pressure. She also had noted significant discomfort in intercourse and slowly increasing menses.

The major feature of the examination was a huge uterus filled with fibroid tumors that occupied the entire pelvis and enough of the abdomen to extend upwards comparable to the displacement of an intrauterine pregnancy of 6 ½ months. With very rare exception, the decision for abdominal hysterectomy would be automatic. The average gynecologist would consider the vaginal route inconceivable.

I had developed the skills required for this type of surgery over the previous 30 years and had removed uteri of this size vaginally several times. Despite the fact that vaginal hysterectomy in the hands of capable surgeons has long been proven to be superior to abdominal hysterectomy in most cases, the overwhelming majority of hysterectomies have been and still are being performed by the latter method. The principal reasons that make the vaginal approach preferable are the speed with which it can be done on average-sized uteri (about 25-30 minutes), the absence of an abdominal wall incision, the non-disturbance of abdominal contents, and the relatively painless and rapid (one-day) recovery regardless of size.

As a result of a longstanding focus on transvaginal uterine removal, particularly in instances of marked enlargement, I had become a national authority in this technique, including the publication of medical journal articles in 1989 and 1999 and the production of two illustrative films that are now housed in the Audio-Visual Library of the American College of Obstetricians and Gynecologists. Based on my experience, I felt that, in Rosemary

Cartland's case, the huge uterine size would not deter successful vaginal extirpation. The operation would take longer, but it could be done. So did we inform the patient and her husband.

One very unusual and decidedly peculiar feature of the examination might have aroused suspicion regarding trouble ahead, but I had decided that it was not a significant impediment to a vaginal procedure. The cervix of the uterus is always readily exposed at the uppermost part of the vagina and, one way or another, is the starting point of any vaginal hysterectomy. The cervix in this case was drawn upwards in a deeply elevated anterior vaginal recess, seemingly almost to the level of the umbilicus (navel), so much so that, combined with the massive pelvic occupation of the main uterus, it could not be seen no matter how deftly I deployed my speculum. I could barely feel it. It was impossible to grasp this cervix and pull it down into a customary position. If we could not do that, then we would be compelled to pursue an abdominal entry through a reasonably large incision with associated disturbance of intra-abdominal contents, and this we wanted to avoid. I cavalierly told my residents that, when the patient was under the relaxing and tension-releasing effects of anesthesia, it would be no problem to shift the cervix appropriately. Or so I thought!

For me, as well as for several of my colleagues, it had become a fairly standard practice in vaginal hysterectomies involving very large fibromyomatous uteri to attempt to reduce the size of the uterus in the four months before the operation. By giving a series of special injections in this time-frame, a remarkable reduction in size can be achieved in a significant number of cases. Of course this makes the surgery easier. It did not work one iota on Rosemary. In all likelihood, we were stuck with a dense, tough, perhaps partially calcified, fibrotic mass that could not respond to the injections and was stuck in the pelvis and abdomen in the weirdest configuration imaginable.

Whenever dealing with cases of this nature, no matter how confident the feeling, one must always obtain the patient's permission in advance to alter to an abdominal entry if unforeseen difficulties demand a change, and this we did with Rosemary. I had never yet had to resort to such a change, however, and did not anticipate it with this case.

On March 3, 1997, we brought Rosemary to the O.R. where, under full general anesthesia, much to my chagrin, disappointment, and disbelief, despite all manner of maneuvers and instrumentation, I was no more successful at dislodging the cervix and bringing it down into view than I had been in the office examining room.

Kira and Ann Marie, my two residents who scrubbed in with me, groaned in unison, "We're going to have to switch and go abdominally. What a shame!"

"You may be right," I responded. Perplexed but undefeated, I took a few moments to think. Suddenly it came to me, admittedly not without trepidation. I knew what to do. "Ladies," I announced, "you are about to participate in an upside down hysterectomy, something I have never seen or heard of before."

With adequate exposure, I made a transverse incision deep in the posterior vagina and entered the abdomen through the posterior pelvis. Then, using scissors and scalpel alternately, beginning at the fundus (top of the uterus) and working from there through the huge corpus (main body of the uterus), I cautiously cut out one series of wedge-shaped slices after another, progressively reducing the huge bulk of tissue until I finally (it seemed like forever because of the tension and apprehension in such a gigantic task) reached the area of the cervix. Elongated and twisted forward and upward some 135°, pointing directly cephalad (toward the patient's head), the cervix was at last brought into view. We disengaged the cervix from its ligamentous attachments and removed it, thereby completing one of the most challenging operations of my career. Wow! We had done the impossible, without significant complication.

We were fortunate that, because of the extremely compact, almost calcific nature of the tissue of the uterine mass, there was negligible bleeding and the two units of blood we had set up for possible transfusion proved unnecessary. This same induration, however, broke six scalpel blades and three pairs of scissors. At the end of the operation, a total of 46 separate pieces of tissue filled two surgical buckets and weighed 1768 grams collectively. Average-sized normal uteri weigh 90-130 grams.

Rosemary ate breakfast the morning after her surgery. Although the operative time was 3 hours and 35 minutes because of the enormous size of the specimen, the patient was on her way home just 22 hours after the last closure stitch. She returned full-time to her job as a receptionist at noon on the fourth post-operative day.

What's that, you say? This story is hard to believe? As Casey Stengel, the old New York Yankee manager, would comment, "You could look it up!" Dr. Raymond A. Lee of the Mayo Clinic, himself a brilliant surgeon, published a report of this case in the January 2000 issue of the Journal of Pelvic Surgery, of which he was editor-in-chief.

Chapter 26
Straight Shooter

"I couldn't possibly feel more miserable," answered Ruth Shapiro to the receptionist's usual query as she registered for her first visit.

Thus began GYN office hours one afternoon in late February 1998, at Temple University Hospital. We soon learned the legitimacy of such a powerfully doleful declaration. This poor lady had endured four major attempts at pelvic reconstructive surgery in the previous 11 years and all had failed completely, leaving her in worse shape afterwards than before, as we soon learned.

Mrs. Shapiro was a 74-year-old married woman who was accompanied on her visit to us by her devoted and concerned husband. Her history revealed good health in every organ system of her body except those directly related to the pelvis. She had experienced three term vaginal deliveries with no apparent associated difficulties. Her problems relevant to loss of pelvic structure and support began after the age of 50 and led to multiple, fruitless procedures aimed at repair. The first one included a vaginal hysterectomy for a prolapsed uterus, and it was all downhill from there.

Since her last operation, almost three years earlier, Ruth had sought help from at least four gynecologic surgeons and two urologists. All of them advised that they could offer nothing that would guarantee any improvement. In fact, they believed that surgery might even worsen her situation. She said the one great stumbling block each of them noted was the absence of a urethra.

"The last doctor who saw me, Dr. Hannon, a urologist, referred me to you. He said you were the only one he knew who might be able to handle all the problems together."

Ruth presented a full gamut of symptoms referable to all three pelvic segments: anterior, middle, and posterior. Certainly there were more than enough symptoms in any one area to reduce the quality of her life to a very low level. However, one symptom stood out well above all the others and was indeed the major source of her misery: "splattering," as she put it.

"I leak a little all the time, without a break, but what really makes life hardly worth living, together with all my other problems, is what happens when I deliberately pee. I splatter urine all over the place, in every direction—on my stockings, on my slip and on a good bit of the floor. I seem to be wet all the time and I can't tell you how many times I change clothes each day. I can't go anywhere and I can't do anything." At this point, she broke down in a convulsion of tears. Her compassionate husband leaned forward and hugged her tightly, sharing completely in her anguish. It was a deeply emotional and stirring scene. I fervently hoped I would be able to figure out some way to help this fine woman when I examined her.

Upon examination, I saw that the moment for decision had arrived. I noticed a very wide introitus (vaginal entry) first. I could fix that. Through it, a severe prolapse of the vaginal vault (vagina turning inside out) came down for almost four inches. I could repair that, too. The bladder bulged markedly down in front and the rectum protruded similarly posteriorly, so both would be amenable to my reconstructive skills. The anal sphincter muscle was severely defective and I envisioned its restoration. Then I faced the real challenge. What Ruth had already told me to expect was true. There was no semblance of a urethra at all, only a hole at the bottom of the bladder marking the site from which the urethra originally began. Urine was leaking from this hole.

The urethra in the adult human female is a muscular tube normally about 3.5 cm (about 1.5 inches) in length that conducts urine from the bladder to the outside. It is supported in elevated angulation at its junction with the bladder in such a way that continence is constant and urinary release from the bladder will occur only upon voluntary effort. When this cystourethral angle is destroyed, the mechanism breaks down and urinary incontinence develops with urine loss appearing only at the urethral meatus, even when there is volitional effort. When there is no urethra at all, even the slightest expulsive exertion can spray urine in all directions. That was Ruth's major problem.

What destroyed Ruth's urethra so completely, creating a rare complication indeed, was the succession of traumatic episodes in her four operations. The operations had progressively eliminated the urethral blood supply, causing its continuous deterioration and ultimately complete disappearance. The bladder muscle surrounding the residual hole adapted to the abnormal situation such that, despite constant leakage, a small volume of urine could be built up over time intervals. When enough urine would accumulate to stir up an urge impulse, the splattering would occur. That is what I confronted. One can perhaps imagine how such a dysfunction could be so destructive to a person's well-being. I had to come up with something and I did.

I placed Ruth on a combined regimen of oral and local estrogen. She massaged the local cream daily into the area immediately surrounding the opening from the bladder, with particular emphasis on the mucosal surfaces on either side of it. I wanted to stir as much life as possible back into those worn and abused tissues, including the underlying muscle and connective tissue as well as the surface mucosa. I told Ruth and her husband that I was sure I could improve her condition but by how much I could offer no guarantees. I explained to them that my primary objective was the creation of a neourethra by some unusual shifting, transferring, and rotating of tissues in combination with judicious employment of synthetic mesh grafts for both strength and sling effects.

Anticipating inquiry from this intelligent couple regarding my previous experience with this type of situation, I beat them to the punch and told them I had "none." I explained that this was an extremely rare complication I had never before seen or heard of, even among my most expertly skilled colleagues. I reassured them, however, that I could make distinct improvements. Having nowhere else to turn, they were willing to gamble one more time. Mr. Shapiro summed things up this way: "Ruth could not be worse off than she already is and she can't go on like this any longer, so we want you to do your best."

On April 10, 1998, I undertook the greatest architectural and anatomical engineering project of my career. For almost six hours, I subjected Ruth Shapiro to the most meticulous set of unusual pelvic maneuvers imaginable, chief among which were 180° reversals of vaginal mucosa and adjacent tissue into a new urethra. Would it work? We held our collective breaths. All my surgical department colleagues had become involved.

Anticipating success, I was compelled to photograph the surgery. If the operation worked, the video would provide a pictorial record of the unique operative methodology for others to follow in the future.

Eureka! In the healing weeks that followed, Ruth's pelvic organs adapted anatomically and functionally beyond all imagination. The splatter was gone! The prolapse was overcome. Bowel function was under control. Most amazingly, we had converted Ruth into a "straight shooter." She voided in a directed stream! Employing militantly measured fluid intake and deliberately voiding every two hours during the day, Ruth essentially eliminated her incontinence. Nocturia was not a problem if fluid intake was curbed after 7 P.M. The Shapiros could not believe the whole thing! Neither could we!

The triumphant "Straight Shooter" video was featured in the 1999 American College of Obstetricians and Gynecologists Annual Film Festival as well as the Emory University GYN Surgical Symposium. It received plaudits at the annual meeting of the Society of Gynecologic Surgeons in 2000 and has been shown at many other professional meetings since then.

Chapter 27
Pick-Up

"I think I'm in early labor, Dr. Grody, but I have a problem getting to the hospital," came the call from Marie diPietro at 3:20 A.M. during a March night in 1969.

"How come?" I asked.

"My husband is on the night shift these days. They're short-handed down there and they've run into some trouble. He will go nuts when I call him. He was hoping this would not happen tonight. Of course, he will come to get me but will he ever be unhappy!"

Marie had been my patient for some years and I had delivered her two other kids. John, her husband, a friendly guy whom I had come to know, was one of the building superintendents of a large local industrial complex.

"Marie, who will watch your kids?"

"That's easy. My next door neighbor is a close friend and she long ago promised to take care of them for me when the time came."

"Then you really have no problem," I reassured her.

"How come?" she countered.

"Because I will pick you up and take you down. You do not live out of the way and I don't think you want to deliver without me. So you can now call your husband and inform him. He can come directly to the hospital from work when he is free. I will get moving while you call John and alert your neighbor.

Shortly thereafter I was helping Marie into the car.

"My friend can't wait to tell everyone that my doctor is personally taking me to the delivery room," she said as she climbed aboard.

Grinning, I said, "When you come home, be sure to tell them I offer this service to all my patients but I charge extra if they break their bag of waters during the ride and mess up my car.

Three hours later, I delivered Marie, just in time for John's arrival.

In my 32 plus years of obstetrical practice, I enjoyed the privilege of transporting patients to the D.R. four times. Nobody delivered in the car. What a story that would have made!

Chapter 28
Point of No Return

"My momma wants me to come back to her, so this is why we want to settle with you today."

Her momma! Can you imagine—a grown woman speaking like that!

Grace Richardson had first come to my office with her husband, Mark, about eleven months previously, in late 1964. They had moved to Manchester, about 16 minutes east of Hartford, four years earlier after moving from Long Island, where they had lived all their lives until Mark's employer relocated him to Connecticut.

After one fruitless year of trying to achieve pregnancy on their own, they had been pursuing that goal under the professional care of Grace's mother's choice of physician on Long Island. Grace's "momma," as she called her, had low regard for and no confidence in gynecologists outside her Long Island sphere, which was associated with North Shore Hospital. So Grace and Mark were making regular trips back and forth between Manchester and Long Island for medical purposes.

When pregnancy had not been achieved after two years of such maneuvering, the Richardsons came to me for help, without telling the domineering mother. I must admit that, on first impression, Mr. Richardson struck me as a creep.

Nevertheless, I applied my normal treatment and Grace subsequently missed her sixth period after initiating her conceptive quest under my aegis. She was rolling along through her fourth month of gestation and booked for delivery at Hartford Hospital. But it was not to be. "Momma" interfered and, at 20 weeks, the blow was struck.

"We are going to have the baby delivered at North Shore Hospital, only a few miles from where my parents live. We can't tell you how grateful we are to you."

"Let me understand," I said. "Mark's job is still in Manchester and you have established permanent residence there, friends and all?" The timid husband was sitting by meek and silent.

"Yes, but please don't think we do not appreciate all you have done for us."

"What baloney! Your mother is well aware of the role I have played. She is not disabled and could easily come and live with you during the few weeks surrounding the expected date of confinement," I stormed at them.

Turning livid, and driving my oral burst at the now cringing, guilt-ridden spouse, I blasted, "And you are returning to the same physician who failed you before!"

I walked around my desk, grasped the patient by the collar as I stood her up, and marched her right through the patient-filled waiting room, Mark sheepishly in tow.

At the door, I wheeled around to him and under the startled gaze of all present, I exclaimed, "You wimp! You know this is wrong and that you should not have let it happen. You are condemned to shame!"

A few moments later, back at work seeing my patients, my ever loyal and understanding office manager, Faith Henry, interrupted me, "Everybody is crazy with curiosity and wants to know what that was all about. What shall I tell them?"

"Don't deprive them. Tell them the truth. They'll love it!"

Four years later, as I sat at my desk preparing for the afternoon agenda, Faith popped in, asking, "Do you remember the Richardsons, that couple you tossed out a few years ago?"

"How could I forget," I answered scornfully.

"Well, you won't believe it, but he's on the phone now. They have not been able to get pregnant again and he wants to know if you will take them back."

"He has to be out of his mind!" I roared.

"He sounds desperate. He says they will pay any fee you ask, in advance. Money is no object."

I responded, "Tell him money is no object with me, either. The answer is 'No.'"

Trying to repress my scorn, I arose, donned my white coat, and walked to the first examining room. The pleasant part of the day, working with my patients, was about to begin.

Chapter 29
Hat's Off!

"Oh, dammit," I exploded to myself. I had just accidentally spilled the specimen onto the metal examining room table. While Martha Ashinsky lay innocently unaware, staring at the ceiling from the gynecologic supine position and waiting for us to place the loaded cap on her cervix, Barbara, my aide, looked on woefully with mouth agape at the mishap. I motioned to her for help as my hands reached like lightning for a tongue depressor to attempt retrieval of the semen concentrate. Had I stupidly blown our very last shot at success? This was the sixth and final month of this capping program.

Martha, 30 years old, had sought pregnancy fruitlessly for several years. She was now completing one year in my care. We had tried everything applicable to the problem she and her husband were experiencing, which was primarily focused on the male factor of oligospermia. In such cases the spermatozoa content of the male ejaculate is inadequate in either or both number and form. Today we were reaching the end of the line.

Cervical capping was a method devised to overcome oligospermia. During my OB/GYN residency at Barnes Hospital and

Washington University, I was fortunate to work with Dr. William H. Masters (of Masters and Johnson fame) in the perfection of this method for solving infertility. Our work in this area culminated in the classic publication, "The Cervical Cap: An Adjunct in the Treatment of Male Infertility," which was published in the Journal of the American Medical Association on May 31, 1952.

In this procedure, the semen specimen, obtained by male manual manipulation, is placed by the gynecologist in a small plastic cap that fits tightly around the cervical opening to the uterus. In this manner, the available spermatozoa are concentrated and protected to afford the best possible chance for insemination, in contrast to natural coital activity. Further enhancement for successful connection is gained, we proved, by using only the initial portion of the ejaculate, which contains almost all of the spermatozoa. Obviously, it is essential that capping be performed in as close as possible a time-frame as the presumptive ovulatory phase indicates, thus oftentimes invoking Sundays and holidays.

Our experience in our study over three years, borne out further in my practice, was that six ovulations were the maximum for capping effect, i.e., if pregnancy was not achieved in that time, capping was not the answer. So here we were, at the sixth and last statistical chance, scraping frantically to recapture those little buggers off the table and into a cap where just one of them might do some good. Bill Ashinsky would not be happy to have to oblige one more time because of my blunder.

Luck! We made it! Oblivious to the extraneous activity, Martha was duly capped, her basal temperature remained elevated, she missed her next nine periods, and, finally, she proved beyond all doubt with the delivery of a healthy full-term daughter at 40 weeks post-capping that life could be launched from a table top. One might appropriately exclaim, with due regard for the capping triumph, "Hats off!"

Chapter 30
Free Samples

"Dr. Grody, I don't want to interrupt you but there's a lady on the phone, calling from New York, who insists on talking to you now. She says it's an extreme emergency."

And it was!

At 1:45 P.M., Wednesday, March 14, 1995, I was immersed in consultations with our residents in the GYN Clinic at Temple University Hospital. We were swamped and I was in no mood for a surprise call from New York. I picked up the phone in the middle of writing a follow-up note.

"Terry, it's Helen Trumbull. I apologize in advance for breaking into your busy schedule like this, especially since you are not going to be at all happy with what I have to tell you. First, I checked and learned that you would be working in your clinic this afternoon. Now I'm sure you remember Martha Williams, the art dealer colleague of mine, whom you met two months ago when you and Sue were in New York and she went out to dinner with us."

"How could I forget her? She's gorgeous, go on, and quickly."

"Because I couldn't make the trip myself, about one hour ago

I put her on a train to Philadelphia to accompany Barbara Roberts, a budding young artist friend of ours who is very sick and who needs to see you at once. I apologize for not calling you in advance because I didn't want to take the chance that you would stop me from sending her down."

This was unreal! I should have been livid, to be so placed in a position of professional vulnerability and responsibility without choice or control. How does the saying go? "Your best friends can be your worst enemies." Yet it was impossible ever to be angry with Helen. There certainly was no more good-hearted and selfless human being on this earth than she. Helen would save the world if she could.

She quickly told me she herself could not make the trip because her own daughter was ill and in the hospital.

"Helen, I don't get it. There are countless sources for good medical care in New York. Why is she coming here?"

"Barbara has no money, no insurance, and no doctor. No one and no place would accept her."

There was no point now in further pursuit of the issue. I was trapped. An unwelcome "guest," a total stranger, led by someone I had met but once before, was being deposited on my doorstep in what soon proved to be extremely dire circumstances.

At 3 P.M. a very alarmed nursing staff introduced me to Barbara Roberts, a specter of humanity supported by a markedly concerned Martha Williams on one side and a grim-faced nurse on the other. All of us have either used or heard the expression, "death warmed over," to describe someone in very bad shape. Well, that's what I saw before me.

Very warmed over, in fact. Barbara was burning with fever. Her temperature was 104.6° F. The abdominal and vaginal examinations revealed a pelvis and lower abdomen locked in the worst case of acute pelvic inflammatory disease of my entire experience. Outside of a hospital bed, I had never seen anyone sicker.

"She needs immediate hospitalization with associated intensive care or she may die," I told both Martha and Barbara. "I can make the arrangements, despite her financial destitution, because of the severity of the case."

The patient had other ideas, however. Her resistance to hospitalization was beyond belief. We made it clear, in the most imperative manner possible, that her life was at stake.

"Please, I must return to New York. I beg of you to load me up with the correct medications and let me go. I will not hold you responsible."

The situation was ridiculous. My responsibility was obvious but I could not persuade the patient, even with Martha pleading fearfully for her to do as I had ordered.

For a fleeting moment I thought of the metaphoric cliché that so many of us might use when others choose a course with which we disagree: "Okay, it's your funeral." Here was a crisis that could not be more applicable to such a phrase, yet where its utterance was precluded by its proximity to a possible real conclusion.

So I had no further recourse than to write down my account of the case, make specific notation of my unqualified recommendation for stat hospitalization, and describe the patient's staunch opposition to my demands. She readily signed a statement affirming her refusal to be admitted, a precaution absolutely necessary to protect both the hospital and me.

Next I went to our free samples closet and put together three distinct, highly potent antibiotic regimens for the patient to follow, of course not knowing which, if any, would work. The retail cost for such a therapeutic outlay would have come to hundreds of dollars.

We gave Barbara the initial doses and then I outlined the program of full therapy and extracted a promise that she would adhere precisely to the schedule. Fluid intake was to be pushed, adequate vitamins were to be taken, nutrition must be forced, and rigid around-the-clock attendance by her friends was critical. She further promised that, if there was no improvement or if she grew worse in the next 24 hours, she would be dropped off in the E.R. of the nearest major hospital without delay. I also told them I wanted a progress call once a day.

Off they went. At 3 P.M. the next day, as I emerged from the O.R., a waiting call from Martha announced remarkably good news. Barbara had responded to the medication as to a bolt from heaven. Her temperature was down to 102.2°, she was taking fluids well, including the traditional chicken soup, and she claimed she was feeling 100% better. She continued on an almost miraculous course to full recovery. Ten days after her visit to Philadelphia, although still somewhat weak, she was back at work in her studio. I received a letter overflowing with gratitude and an invitation to her studio so Sue and I could choose a painting.

About four months later, during a weekend visit to Helen Trumbull, we found our way to Barbara Roberts' studio. In the meantime, she had sold four paintings through Helen and Martha, had become financially solvent, had enrolled in a Blue Cross/Blue Shield program, and was being followed by a gynecologist of my recommendation. Sue selected a beautiful 6' x 7' abstract painting that now graces the east wall of our dining room.

Shakespeare might have commented, "All's Well That Ends Well."

Chapter 31
Breaking Waters

Oh, no! It was happening again. The cervix, for the third pregnancy in a row, was silently effacing, with the bag of waters just starting to bulge through the internal opening of the cervix. The cervix was shortened almost to 2 centimeters (normal is 3 centimeters) and was dilated just enough to allow palpation of the bulging bag of waters. The pregnancy was only at 19 weeks, far too early for viability.

Francine McAllister's regular obstetrician sent her to us in the above condition for consultation and further management. He was quite upset with himself for not having acted earlier with the performance of a cerclage procedure to counteract what the patient's sorrowful pregnancy history indicated was a case of an incompetent cervix. An incompetent cervix is one that is too weak structurally to hold an intrauterine pregnancy intact through the full 40 weeks of gestation.

The patient herself, deeply immersed in the prospects of motherhood and facing failure for her third consecutive attempt, was, as you can imagine, almost hysterical. Intense counseling was in order at once, combined with immediate operative intervention, in a last-ditch effort to save the pregnancy. First, confronting the likelihood that she would not be able to carry the fetus to the point of viability, we reasoned with Francine that she was only 25 years old and that, by advance prophylactic cerclage surgery, we almost certainly could prevent a bad outcome the next time. This afforded a modicum of consolation. Second, we would now perform a simple emergency procedure on her cervix that, with prayer and loads of good luck, might give us a remote chance of carrying the current gestation reasonably further.

We went to the operating room within hours of first meeting and examining the patient. We felt that it was too late, at almost 20 weeks, to chance a full cerclage closure of the cervix. Instead we opted for something we had picked up from the Australian obstetrical literature. This consisted of the placement of two heavy-bore non-absorbable through-and-through cervical sutures, one anterior-posterior and one transverse. These were positioned at the approximate level of the normal inner (upper) opening of the cervical canal, three centimeters above the outer opening. The sutures were tied as the slightly bulging bag of waters was digitally displaced upward above the ensuing closure. They would be cut at the very outset of true labor. Next came the waiting game.

After two quiescent days of hospital bed rest, Francine was sent home on a strict regimen of very limited activity. She was warned to remain recumbent except for bathroom necessities and meals. She was seen in the office at 21 weeks and 24 weeks, displaying normal progress in the pregnancy. A very concerned husband and sister were enormously helpful.

We all waited … and hoped.

At 25 weeks she began leaking small amounts of amniotic fluid. Exam with sterile speculum verified our worst fears. The bag of waters had developed a tiny leak. The jig was up. The only sensible course now was to cut the sutures and let the pregnancy unload.

Discussing the situation with the patient and her husband, I explained in no uncertain terms that any attempt now to continue the pregnancy, even though the break in the bag of waters was probably minimal, would place her life in jeopardy. The potential for infection was great, and if that occurred under such closed circumstances, lethal risks would be tremendous.

Francine's decision was immediate. There was no hesitancy. "I am going to go for it, no matter what," she said. "If I just give up, I will never get over it." Her husband, though reluctant, felt he had no choice but to support her.

We documented everything in writing. The McAllisters both signed legal documents taking responsibility for their decision. We needed more fingers to be crossed than we had available.

A visiting nurse came by daily to check the pregnancy, i.e., fetal heartbeat, fetal movement, and uterine growth, plus Francine's temperature. Amazingly, everything proceeded as though nothing unusual had happened despite continued mild leaking of amniotic fluid. Uterine growth followed a normal pattern. We held our collective breath, hoping to get to 28 weeks, at the least, without trouble.

At 29 ½ weeks, true labor began. No sign of infection had ever developed. Gerald McAllister raced his wife to the hospital where we immediately cut the retaining cervical sutures. Labor progressed evenly under epidural analgesia and was terminated with the very gentle forceps delivery of a healthy normal 2 pound 15 ounce female dubbed Geraldine. Congratulations were offered and accepted all around!

Two years later we performed an interim cervical cerclage procedure to reduce the chance that the next pregnancy would end with an early miscarriage.

Three years later we delivered Caroline McAllister at 38 weeks by cesarean section.

When last heard from, Geraldine was a top student in the third grade.

Sometimes luck beats out good sense.

Chapter 32
Fertilizer

"Dr. Grody, I have a funny story to tell you," said Catherine Bellhorn to me as we sat in my office after her annual physical exam.

Catherine was a recently retired English teacher from the West Hartford public school system. She lived in nearby Farmington where, she had told me in the past, she and her husband owned about one-and-one-half acres.

"Joe and I are going to have some fun and become amateur farmers and put our land to work. It's been idle long enough and we now have the time."

"Sounds like a great way to enter retirement," I commented.

"We were given expert advice to increase the arable quality of our soil first in order to give us a better yield. So we searched through the relevant news sources for a place to buy fertilizer. We found what we wanted, climbed into our pickup and headed for the shit farm."

I couldn't believe my ears! Mrs. Bellhorn was as refined and proper a woman as I ever had in my entire practice. True, I could have been mistaken—she spoke softly and rapidly. All I could do, dumbfounded, was nod. Some funny story!

Catherine continued, "We arrived at the shit farm and there to greet us herself was Mrs. Schiff." The light hit me! The Schiff farm was loaded with livestock, furnishing a rich supply of fertilizer. It was not illogical, all things considered, to think that, when one wanted fertilizer, a shit farm would be the place to go to, even though it was difficult to imagine advertising the stuff as such. The ad actually stated that the Schiff Farm was selling fertilizer. My wild interpretation of Catherine's rapidly delivered, slightly slurred diction certainly evoked a four-letter Anglo-Saxon word not likely to appear in her usual vocabulary.

So where was the funny story? "Eleanor Schiff and I began chatting and we learned that we both had the same gynecologist—you."

Then I told Catherine Bellhorn what I thought she had said and we laughed hysterically. It was indeed a funny story.

Chapter 33
SIDS

Tears flowed unrelentingly. Her shoulders ached from the endless sobbing. Her world was shattered. Just two months previously she had been bursting with joy at the sound of her newborn son's first cries. Now, suddenly, he was dead.

Maria DiBattista was as delightful and charming a young lady as we had ever seen in our office. Her sparkling dark eyes and the warmth of her ever-present smile made her regular prenatal visits a joy for all of us. At 21 years, she could not wait to join her four siblings in parenthood. Ramon, her equally ebullient husband, who was a teacher in the Hartford public school system, added even more to the pleasant experience of her office visits.

Maria did beautifully with a normal pregnancy and an uncomplicated vaginal delivery and immediate postpartum course. She brought her newborn son with her at her six week checkup where he was smothered with all the usual "oos" and "ahs."

Two weeks later, Ramon, crying profusely, called me. "Jorge is dead," he sobbed. He had been smothered again, this time the real thing, in his crib, a case of what is now referred to as SIDS

(Sudden Infant Death Syndrome). No greater grief can confront a young couple.

We had Ramon bring Maria to the office at once. Understandably she was inconsolable. But my partners and I and our nursing personnel were her trusted friends who loved her. She needed us now and we would not let her down.

Over the next eight weeks, in one way or another, all of us counseled Maria and Ramon from the depths of our hearts on four separate visits. We judiciously and patiently plowed through every line of reasoning with them. We convinced them to start over immediately.

Our collective homespun counseling was successful. Maria conceived again after three periods. Intense anti-SIDS training took place. In timely fashion, a daughter was born. Two years later a son was added. There were no complicating circumstances of any kind. When last heard from, two DiBattista children, at 8 and 6 years, were doing just fine. Happiness reigned!

Could such a scenario occur again in today's austere and impersonal clinical world? Not likely! Maria and Ramon would be referred to a psychologist, a totally new person, whose approach, no matter how skillfully conducted, could never match our empathy and heartfelt warmth because of the relationship we had previously established. And the financial aspect would present a tremendous burden, an additional negative psychological factor. Our counseling was provided at no charge. We felt it was our responsibility to act as we did. Our payoff was the subsequent happy ending.

Chapter 34
We Took It Out and Sent Her Home

"I admit I'm vain, but from what I've read, I'm sure it can be done." So claimed this 34-year-old, single, very assertive woman who registered in the Temple University Hospital private GYN clinic one Wednesday morning in January 1999.

Irene Makosky presented a two-year history of progressively increasing and moderately disabling symptoms of pelvic pressure and functional pelvic interference. She had been told her condition was caused by a very large fibroid tumor occupying the entire posterior wall of the uterus, filling the space between the cervix and the rectum and compressing both the upper vagina and the rectum. This could be demonstrated objectively by both examination and ultrasonogram. The patient brought the USG images with her.

I was the ninth (!) gynecologist Irene visited for this problem. She readily accepted the need for surgery to remove the tumor. The route to be taken for the surgery concerned her, however. Primarily, she wanted to avoid hysterectomy, which would have provided an easy and quite definitive solution to her problem, because she hoped to bear children in the future. Also, she felt, from her personal search of gynecological literature, that the myomectomy (the name of the required operation) could be done without the routine incision through the abdominal wall (laparotomy).

Specifically, Irene was hoping for surgery by laparoscopy (via a metal tube through a very small and inconspicuous abdominal wall entry) or through the vagina. According to the patient, all previous opinions precluded laparoscopy because of the deep location of such a large tumor behind the uterus. Additionally, she said that all eight physicians admitted to no experience at vaginal myomectomy and had told her they felt it would be very difficult to perform anyway through a nulliparous pelvis, i.e., one where the tissues had not been stretched and relaxed by previous vaginal delivery of a term infant. In essence, Irene was informed that she had no choice other than a standard abdominal laparotomy. The last doctor she saw referred her to me as the one he knew with the most experience in such a situation.

I examined Irene and found essentially the anatomic condition she had depicted. Using the USG image as a prop, I described for her the uterus as an upside-down Bartlett pear and the fibroid as a cantaloupe that had completely occupied the entire posterior part of the pear. I informed Irene that I was reasonably certain I could perform the vaginal myomectomy she was seeking without remarkable difficulty but that I might have to make a small lateral perineal incision, which would never have reason to come into public view, if the anesthesia did not provide enough pelvic muscle relaxation to allow for adequate operative exposure through the vaginal entrance.

Three weeks later, with excellent anesthesia and first class assistance from a fellow and a resident, I performed the requisite intra-abdominal surgery through a three-centimeter transverse incision deep in the posterior vagina behind the cervix. The lateral perineal incision was not necessary. The operation consisted of a succession of wedge-shaped tissue excisions until the tumor was completely extricated. Blood loss was limited to less than two tablespoonfuls by the judicious use of vasoconstrictive injections into the tumor site during the operation. The residual defect of the surgery was closed in two suture layers, after which the uterus appeared to be totally normal by both palpation and vision. Both ovaries and both tubes were incidentally viewed as healthy and normal.

The operation required only 58 minutes. The cumulative tumor mass weighed 169 grams. The estimated uterine weight, from both palpation at surgery and later ultrasonographic images, was a normal 100 grams.

The operation was performed early in the morning. The patient was discharged to home at the end of the day on Tylenol as necessary.

This operation was filmed as an educational video production. Under the title, "Vaginal Myomectomy: No Laparotomy, No Laparoscopy," it was featured at the Emory Hospital Film Festival in 1999 and at the annual meeting of the Society of Gynecologic Surgeons and the annual Film Festival of the American College of Obstetricians and Gynecologists in 2000. It sits now in the Audio-Visual Library of the latter organization and has been shown at numerous locations.

(Message to other gynecologists: you can do it, too!)

Chapter 35
Doubling Up

Who says you can't have it both ways? Two vaginas! Wow, how lucky can one be!

Irene Livingston came to my office as a new obstetric patient in the third month of her second pregnancy. According to her history, her first delivery, in another city, had occurred by cesarean section because of cephalopelvic disproportion (vertex not capable of fitting through the bony maternal pelvis).

The patient almost immediately informed me, before any exam, that she had two vaginas. I verified this anatomic peculiarity a short time later and gained the impression, from observable and palpable signs, that this was a right-sided pregnancy. On questioning, Irene told me she thought she remembered that her previous obstetrician had indicated right uterine gestation also on the first occasion. (We later found this to be so in her records sent to us, on our request, from her previous hospital.)

A persistent dual genital tract in an otherwise anatomically normal human female is singularly uncommon. Such a condition results from incomplete fetal development. In the very early female fetus, duplicate genital tracts exist side by side. Gradual intrauterine progress normally leads to a fusion phenomenon in which the lower thirds of these tracts form a single vagina and the middle thirds a single cervix and uterus. The uppermost thirds remain separate as the Fallopian tubes, one on each side of the pelvis in juxtaposition to the ovary of that side. When fusion does not occur, as it obviously had not in Irene, pregnancy may occur in either uterus and proceed to term.

A repeat cesarean section was scheduled. The pregnancy proceeded in routine fashion, but my imagination took off. Here I was presented with a rare situation for practical fertility control. First, I determined by both examination and consultation with Irene and her husband that the left vagina was as coitally efficient and satisfying as the right. Then I proposed that, simultaneously with the cesarean section, I tie off the left tube. Irene would then become the world's most unique and ideal woman: right side for procreation, left side for recreation! They loved the concept. No more birth control pills. If they wanted another child, it would be a simple matter of anatomic flip-flop. All that mattered was leaving no margin for careless selection on celebratory occasions when "under the influence."

All went well. The section delivery of a robust term male from the right uterus occurred on schedule. The left tube was tied.

In the ensuing four years before the Livingstons moved again, there was no evidence that the workshop was ever confused with the playground.

It was the best of ties.

Chapter 36
Confrontation with Death: An Insider's View

Dawn arrived on Monday, December 20, 2004, and with it came, automatically, my diurnal grateful reflections on a rewarding life. Here I stood, at 82 years, still productive at what I did best. A few months ago my wonderful wife and I had celebrated our fiftieth wedding anniversary with our extended family participating in our joy. Sue and I would now conclude this memorable year in spectacular fashion with our acknowledgement of her 75th birthday over six days in Washington and New York starting on December 24. Meanwhile, our three children and their families would, as usual in the winter holiday vacation time, enjoy skiing together at our chalet at Stratton Mountain, Vermont. How fortunate I was!

I was a survivor with no end in sight. My blood pressure and P.S.A. were both low, my EKG was perfect, and my latest chest x-ray showed no negative residuals from a previous hemi-pneumonectomy. My hands remained steady as a rock and my daily assaults on *The New York Times* crossword puzzle met with unwavering success. Cancer, cardiovascular catastrophes, and automobile calamities were not in my portfolio. No, sir. I was the doctor. Others were patients, but not me.

Or so I thought!

Indeed, today would be a critical day to get work done in my office. The holiday season was on, no clinic hours were scheduled, and planning for our blockbuster surgical conference in June was about to transform from well-conceived outline into frenzied reality. I had made a commitment on which I was obligated to deliver. The previous July, I had persuaded the Robert Wood Johnson Medical School Department of Obstetrics and Gynecology to host a major international medical conference, a complex and costly venture with considerable financial risk. It had not been easy. Although I had successfully organized numerous conferences in the past and was supremely confident that this one, too, would be a smashing success, my enthusiasm and ebullience initially were not sufficient to overcome the trepidation of Dr. Ronald Jaffe, our department chairman. Nonetheless, I was determined to organize one last major clinical scientific meeting as my legacy and ultimate professional contribution and he eventually succumbed to my assurances of success.

The project would demand not only my time but my organizational expertise. June was not as far off as it seemed. In fact, not a moment could be spared, especially since my regular clinical and teaching activities would continue unabated during the planning time frame. God forbid that anything might interfere with my grand blueprint. Not the least of my concerns was that we had signed a contract for many thousands of dollars with the Hyatt Hotel, the only meeting place that would allow us to bring in the cadavers that were to be a highlight of the conference.

Arriving at the hospital on this busy day, I hit the ground running. I conducted an exhilarating morning planning session that finished with our sights focused on 9 A.M. the following morning, when we would begin the arduous task of screening more than 200 videos of gynecological procedures to cull the 65 or so that we would use in our conference.

At midday, I consumed my usual tuna fish sandwich, and, at 12:45 P.M., started on my usual postprandial trip to the restroom. From that point on, nothing was "usual" ever again.

In the midst of my evacuating mission, I suddenly became dizzy, not a regular side effect of this mundane activity. As I returned to my desk perplexed, I noticed mild chest discomfort that continued unabated for the next thirty minutes. "This is probably just a little indigestion," I conjectured, and I continued to write and read. Figuring that some buffering effect might alleviate the symptoms, I withdrew a cookie from my bottom drawer "nosh" collection and ate it. Many moments passed without amelioration. Actually, my discomfort was increasing. I finally decided that enough was enough. I was coming down with something and would be best off at home in bed despite the time pressure from the upcoming conference.

So I called Sue to tell her that I wasn't feeling so hot and would be driving home early. I would not be picking her up from her office on the way home as I usually did. I then pulled myself together and headed for the staircase. Why did going down the single flight seem like such an effort today? Walking toward the garage suddenly became a distinct chore. As I pushed the button to open the door to the hospital garage, I realized, now with more than a tinge of fright, that I was much sicker than I wanted to accept.

I never made it through the door. Experiencing real chest pain, I abruptly about-faced, lumbered into the elevator, and made a beeline for the office of Dr. Edward Viner, my internist, who also served as chairman of the Department of Medicine. Upon arrival,

I immediately announced to the receptionist that I was seriously ill and needed Dr. Viner at once. The two medical associates present, stirred into action by my startling proclamation and the look of fright on my now pallid countenance, whipped me into an examining room and began checking my vital signs and setting up for an electrocardiogram as Dr. Viner burst in.

He quickly reviewed my history, which revealed no evidence of prior or premonitory cardiovascular disease. I was tapped out and listened to, my blood pressure was checked in both arms, and a full-scale EKG was performed. Amazingly, everything appeared normal and reassuring, but my non-radiating deep chest pain persisted and seemed to be slowly worsening. Fortunately, the hero of the moment, Dr. Viner, had swung his diagnostic antennae into high gear. He called for the medical cardiac team to come running, he ordered a stat echocardiogram of the heart and ascending aorta, he alerted the cardiac surgical group to be ready for possible urgent participation, and he ordered arrangements for stat hospital admission. Then he had me call Sue at her office. It was 3 P.M.

Luck is a relative thing. Suddenly confronting an unknown, but clearly very serious, danger, I found myself, peculiarly, celebrating my good fortune. The place was right: Cooper University Hospital. The time was right: daytime regular weekday working hours. Coincidental conflicting hospital crises: none. The right personnel: all the key people were available; no one was ill; no one was on vacation; no one was tied up. Everything was ready, should an accident happen.

The most serendipitous circumstance, however, proved to be an event that had occurred in the hospital only hours before my problem manifested itself. At 7:30 A.M. that same day, the medical Grand Rounds conducted under Dr. Viner's aegis had discussed the syndrome of dissecting aortic aneurysm as its core topic. As a result, the Cooper University Hospital Department of Medicine could not have been more thoroughly alert to the signs and symptoms that define this major vascular catastrophe. Who could have imagined that their training would so quickly be put to the test?

We reached Sue at her Philadelphia office and I told her that Dr. Viner was admitting me to the hospital as a patient. Reflecting on the conversation later, I recall having been particularly concerned that she be able to locate our automobile in the hospital garage. At some point, Dr. Viner took over the phone and, disguising his diagnostic premonition, told her he was placing me under observation pending further testing results. "You needn't bother coming over till 5 or 5:30 when things will be more definitive," he said to her. Obviously, he didn't know to whom he was talking, for Sue was bouncing from her chair and heading for the door even as she placed the telephone back in its cradle. As she told me later, she remembered and understood the full meaning of those words, "For better and for worse, for richer or for poorer, in sickness and in health." More than one vow was in play.

Sue arrived to find a room teeming with people: staff physicians, residents, technicians, nurses, students. Sue huddled close by me as Dr. Viner approached us, a dark scowl etched on his face and medical documentation in his hand. The Grim Reaper in a scrub suit. "We now have a definite diagnosis," he pronounced. "The echocardiogram confirms what I suspected from the start. You have an acute dissecting aortic aneurysm."

My aorta was splitting open? Oh. And the day had started off so brightly. This sounded horrible. As I inquired about the prognosis, I was assured that it could not have been more so.

"You will require stat surgery," Dr. Viner intoned, in synch with the nods of the multiple heads of the consulting medical cardiac group. "Terry, I already alerted Dr. Jonathan Cilley about the probable need for his services. I am calling him so his team can take over this case immediately. Trust me." Those last two words were frightening. They seemed to beg the disquieting question of why trust was necessary under the circumstances. They failed to convey the intended reassurance.

"Who is Dr. "Silly?"" Sue and I asked in unison.

"He is a top-flight cardiovascular surgeon. He heads up the team that will operate on you," answered Dr. Viner. Sue and I said nothing.

Shortly thereafter, Dr. Jonathan Cilley materialized, accompanied by his own entourage, and, to our relief, looking every bit as serious as Dr. Viner. After brief introductory words, he informed us that he had reviewed the history and all the pertinent clinical information. Then, Dr. Cilley began his examination of my chest. Dr. Viner watched him intently while the medical cardiologists and the cardiac surgeons looked on and discussed the situation.

Completing his examination, Dr. Cilley, sat down, facing patient and spouse, to explain the stark facts and the terrible risks I faced. "You were fortunate that this aortic dissection happened in these circumstances or you would have died," he said. Lucky me, I mused. He went on, "However, that was only the first hurdle. The lethal probabilities during the surgery are not insignificant."

Aha! The ploy of the clever physician: euphemistic circuitry. I long ago contrived this title for the method many doctors use to make medical crises sound far less harsh than they are. But his trick did not succeed. "You mean, Jonathan, that there's a dammed good chance I can die during the operation?"

"Yes, exactly," he answered.

"Suppose I elect to forego the surgery—then what?" I retorted.

"Then you will surely die," came back his emphatic response.

Obviously, I had no choice.

Then it got worse. "I must tell you also, Terry, that this defect is in the most vulnerable area of the aorta, the ascending portion. In such cases, in surviving victims (he really said patients but that's not what I heard) we often find evidence of cerebral compromise."

Again with the euphemistic circuitry. "You mean that, if I make it, I could be a vegetable?"

"Bluntly speaking, yes," he answered.

On that cheery note, he set the operating room into high gear. Nurses moved in with medications. The anesthesiologists began to prepare for the impending surgery.

It was now after 6 P.M. Sue was on the telephone, frantically trying to locate our three children: Erica in New York, Miles in Potomac, MD, and Jeffrey in Hartford, CT.

Watching helplessly, I confronted mortality. Was this really it? My usually hyperactive imagination was flying wildly, with fear catalyzing thoughts that were anything but sublime. Was my whole life racing before me? No. I was not ready for this—I still had too much to do. I always make plans, and this was not in my current blueprint.

I certainly would not be able to tend to unfinished business as a vegetable. What kind of vegetable anyway? Broccoli, string bean, carrot? What about celery to satisfy residual lusty dreams? I could just see it happening: the produce manager at Genuardi's saying, as he points me out, "That used to be a brilliant surgeon for women's problems, but now he is the best head of lettuce in the store."

Was the medication getting to me this quickly? If ever there was occasion for me to be removed from reality, this was it, and the pre-op medications, thank goodness, were doing the job.

Sue began to locate the children. It was time to say good-bye. As she turned up each one in succession, tears flowed freely. For the next half hour, the telephonic lines dripped with melodramatic expressions between parent and child. "I love you" again and again, "perfect dad," "wonderful children," "what pride I have had in you," "we have had so much fun," "the memories will never leave us," "I could not have picked a better family," and on and on.

Suddenly, good-byes ended and it was time for business. The clock read 8 P.M. I was placed on a cart, now completely succumbing to the sedative effects of the drugs. From far away, the kids were making plans to join Sue. In the midst of all the tumult, Sue realized she would have to race home briefly to care for our Maltese pup.

The hospital staff trundled me off to the operating room, where my body was prepared for surgery, I was stuck with needles, IV's were started, and a catheter was inserted into you-know-where. Shortly after 9 P.M. the anesthesia team shunted me to dreamland and bodily destruction began as my sternum was hacked open down the middle to expose the inner workings of my chest.

The surgical procedure included total cardiac bypass, cannulation of the right coronary atrium and certain major blood vessels, draining out the blood from my body, locating the dissection point in the aorta, clamping the ascending aorta and then opening the aorta over the tear in the aortic arch. With no blood in my body, my critical life functions were performed by a heart-lung machine for 46 minutes while Dr. Cilley and his team worked. Repair of the damaged aorta was effected by fashioning a Dacron fabric graft patch that was attached to the aortic wall by a substance called bio-glue, supplemented by sutures. When this was completed, the aorta was unclamped, my heparinized blood was returned to its normal tunneled environs, my heart spontaneously (!) returned to its normal rhythm, and "surgical closure was performed in standard manner."

Wow! When I read the operative report after I returned home,

I was amazed. Competitor that I am, I couldn't help but compare my own operative masterpieces as a gynecological reconstructive surgeon with the challenges Dr. Cilley had faced. The comparison was humbling. Clearly, I concluded, what Dr. Cilley and others like him accomplish surgically is far more important and impressive than even the most seemingly miraculous procedures we pelvic reconstructive surgeons perform. The complex and intricate maneuvers demanded of them allow no margin for error. Had Dr. Cilley slipped up just once while operating on me, I could have been a dead duck (or a live vegetable). In contrast, if any part of my operative endeavors fails, life is not threatened, and usually there is another chance to overcome the failure. Not so when vital organs, like the heart and the aorta, are involved. All hail to life-savers like Dr. Cilley!

Of course, my reflections on Dr. Cilley's surgical prowess occurred much later, after consciousness returned. In the meantime, while I was "under the knife," Sue was all alone in the O.R. waiting room, a location typically crammed with patients' relatives and friends in the daylight hours, but occupied in the solitary darkness of wee morning hours only by anxious and frightened family members hanging on edge, hoping the surgeon will come out soon with good news. Erica arrived at 2 A.M. As Dr. Cilley emerged at about 3:30 A.M. to announce that I was in stable condition in the intensive care unit, Miles appeared. Jeff, who had remained at home in Hartford with plans to arrive shortly, was contacted and informed that funeral arrangements had been postponed, at least for the time being.

I was oblivious to everything, of course. For twenty-four hours—from Tuesday morning until the beginning of the following day, I was later told—I lay semi-conscious and in a blur as countless colleagues, staff doctors, nurses, and aides came by to check my progress or otherwise to assist. I was moved from the Cardiac Intensive Care Unit to the regular cardiac care floor. Amidst the gibberish that escaped my lips from time to time, observers discerned occasional pleas that I be allowed to return to the office to work on my videos for the upcoming conference. Delirious though I was, this nonsense probably was the first real sign that my mental faculties might return to their pre-operative condition. Thus, as Wednesday unfolded, the prognosis looked good and my family began to relax.

Not for long, however. Later Wednesday, I went completely haywire, apparently in response to the post-operative medications. Suddenly, my vital signs deteriorated and I started thrashing about wildly, pulling out I.V. needles and throwing my arms and legs all over the place. They later claimed that I even tried to yank out my Foley catheter. Optimism vanished in the space of a few hours. Jeffrey was instructed to head to Philadelphia without delay. My brother, in South Carolina, who had plans to fly up on Thursday, was directed to catch the next plane instead.

Fortunately, a bright young physician on the Cooper cardiac care team jumped to the rescue. Her expeditious dispensation of an antidote reversed my deterioration. Jeffrey stayed with me Wednesday night and by Thursday morning, I had returned from never never land to the real world. Awakening, I was greeted by the tearful but smiling faces of my wife, my three children, and my brother, Allan. Not yet aware of the events that had transpired since Monday afternoon, my first words, directed at Allan, were, "What are you doing here?"

They gradually brought me up to date on all that had happened. While doing so, they assisted with a variety of simple tasks that previously I had performed for myself. Jeffrey shaved me with my own electric razor, Erica brushed my teeth, and Miles fed me lunch, Sue helped bathe me, and Allan filled me in on the latest off-season dealings of the Phillies and Red Sox. Swarms of aides, nurses, and physicians, including Drs. Cilley and Viner and Dr. Fred Ginsberg, a cardiologist, circulated in and out all day.

They pronounced that I was now likely to survive.

Capping an upbeat Thursday afternoon was the arrival of a warm handwritten note from Katie Couric, then co-host of NBC's "Today" show, bearing wishes for a full and speedy recovery. Katie interviewed me in August, 2000 and we had stayed in touch afterwards. Learning of my trauma, she took the time from her hectic schedule to wish me well. Although I was still very much in a fog about real events, what a shot of adrenalin that was!

Friday, December 24, was Sue's 75th birthday. Instead of romping around Washington with me visiting museums and galleries and dining in fine restaurants, there she sat at my bedside. Although she had been informed that I was likely to be okay, she knew there were no guarantees and she could tell that I was not out of the woods by any means. So, she spent her special birthday by my side, sending our three children and my brother out for dinner. Concerned as everyone was about my condition, they all forgot the occasion and didn't even bring dinner for her. I stole my wife's 75th birthday! Later, when I learned what had happened, I vowed that I would make it up to her.

Finally, on the eighth post-op day, I was rolled out of Cooper University Hospital in an unaccustomed conveyance (wheelchair) to face the world again, albeit from an unanticipated vantage point. I determined not to mope. Having been offered a chance to stick around awhile longer, I knew I had to make the most of it. One immediate and unfortunate change was unavoidable, however. Suddenly, I had transitioned from my accustomed role as Sue's companion to a new role, of undefined duration, as her burden. It is under these circumstances, more than any other, that one fully appreciates the benefits and advantages of having married "well" in the only sense that matters!

Newly discharged from the hospital, and clearly not back to my old self physically, I was eager to determine the extent of any damage that might have been inflicted on my mental functions. I put myself to the test right away and, to my immense relief, passed. Despite difficulty with the physical act of speaking, I was delighted to conclude that my intellectual agility appeared to be alive and well. What better way for a physically challenged recuperating patient to test his mind than to attack *The New York Times* daily crossword puzzles! That small activity did much not only to help me pass the time but also to regain confidence that, in the most important respects, I was unscathed by my ordeal.

Next on my personal assessment schedule was memory. I did not need physicians to tell me that the significant cerebral oxygen deprivation I had experienced could jeopardize my ability to recall both old and recent events. To my amazement, my memory of almost everything seemed, if anything, to be even more acute and vivid than it had been before. The cacophony of life experiences that had not "flashed by" as I prepared to go under the knife, now confronted me, cascading before me in waves of recollection that encompassed both consequential and trivial memories. This occurred even though I made no deliberate effort to promote the phenomenon. Remembrances of every sort—triumphs, embarrassments, happiness, tears, recent events and distant childhood recollections—all swept by. It was a strange and unprecedented experience for me. Most assuredly, it was wonderful to go back with clarity to the age of three years (!) but it was disturbing to face, along with the pleasant reminiscences, embarrassing, humiliating, stupid, and ugly occurrences that I thought had been erased from my consciousness forever. I was curious whether others placed in similar dire circumstances encountered the same flashback phenomenon. Whatever the answer, it occurred to me that, no matter what else was going on, my memory was not impaired. The real proof occurred when my mind returned to the need to continue planning for the major surgical conference coming up in June, in exactly the way I had been involved prior to my accident.

So, assessing myself post-discharge, I concluded that mentally I was unaffected by what had occurred but that physical recovery would be necessary. I had definitely lost some ambulatory capabilities and some of my sense of balance. My caring physicians issued universally rosy predictions that these physical deficiencies would disappear over a period of weeks, but that did not happen. I remained confined to a "walker" for mobility even though I underwent an intensive and well-managed program of physiotherapy. For some time, there seemed to be minimal perceptible improvement, including my sense of balance; not all that encouraging, but at least there were no signs of regression. Using my new psychological weapon—rationalization—I noted that I was still alive, acting cognitively, and able to contribute. That is when I began writing this memoir.

On a Sunday almost five weeks after my operation, I registered a most curious problem. Sitting at my desk at noontime writing a medical case report, I heard Sue call from the kitchen, one floor below, to tell me that lunch was ready. As I rose from my chair, I attempted to answer her but could produce only guttural, unintelligible sounds. Although my thoughts were all in order, the harder I tried to speak, the worse it became. It was terribly frightening. There was no warning, no headache, no feeling of faintness, and no loss of consciousness. I was even able to work myself downstairs. But no intelligible sounds came through.

Naturally, Sue was on the phone at once to track down Dr. Viner. While we were waiting, I regained, very slowly, the ability to form one-syllable words. By 2 P.M., Dr. Viner was grilling me on the telephone with the standard litany of simple questions about identity, time, and place that medical professionals use to draw a quick bead on a patient's mental state. He concluded that my cerebral function remained intact but postulated a diagnosis of TIA, i.e., transient ischemic attack, another term I had not heard before. Dr. Viner explained that TIAs, sometimes referred to as "mini-strokes" or "warning strokes," occur when a blood clot temporarily clogs an artery, preventing part of the brain from obtaining blood. TIAs clear quickly, unlike real strokes, and do not leave lasting injury to the brain or residual symptoms. He said they are not uncommon in people of my age, but, in my case, considering my recent debacle, Dr. Viner wisely felt that immediate neurological consultation and imaging were in order. He was worried that something slightly more ominous, like a minor stroke, had occurred despite the absence of symptoms other than my speech impairment.

So, he rounded up Dr. Mitra Assadi, a young hotshot of the Cooper Neurological Department, and, in her care, I spent five hours in the crowded Cooper Hospital Emergency Room. She gave me a thorough neurological exam and ordered an MRI. All the results were within normal limits. Repeat exams and tests were performed over the next several weeks without yielding definitive findings. Eventually, they concluded that I had, in fact, sustained a stroke because my diction, although comprehensible when I labored at clear articulation, never returned to anything close to my crisp, pre-operative rapid-fire delivery and also because I never was able to escape the necessity of a walker for mobility.

If there was good news, it was that the neurological interference was clearly a motor issue only. Mental acuity and associated cerebral activity and stamina were never compromised. Thus, although I realized, much to my chagrin, that I would never again attend patients directly and that my days as a surgeon were over, I took heart from the fact that I was able to continue arranging educational programs and participating personally in Grand Rounds lecture sessions. Most of all, and much to the relief of Dr. Jaffe, our OB/GYN chairman, I was thrilled that I remained fully able to pour my energies into the final arrangements for the June pelvic reconstructive surgical conference.

Obviously, as I was forced to accept unforeseen and unwelcome changes, Sue was, too. With her continual assistance, I faced all the routine aspects of daily life with customary vigor, despite my infirmities, determined to carry on as though nothing unusual had happened. Before my calamity occurred, however, I was able to do those things without her assistance. Now, I not only was largely unable to help with household chores, I suddenly became a significant burden on my spouse. The number one issue was my balance. Regrettably, Viagra does not help the kind of erection I had trouble maintaining, which was the ability to stay on my feet, without falling, while moving about the house. Sue and I learned that any effort I made to get around the house with my walker could lead to a dangerous fall, meaning that Sue had to be present and "on alert" at all times, which imposed a serious strain on her.

Although Sue's vigilance prevented many topples, some occurred despite her efforts. For a while, I averaged about two per week, leading to a succession of bruises and contusions of varying severity in diverse body locations. Luckily, fractures were limited to one episode involving three lower left ribs, which, although quite uncomfortable for several days, caused no lasting damage. Finally, we decided that an aide needed to be present whenever Sue was not, another undesired surrender to the exigencies of my situation and a further loss of independence.

I was very fortunate that I had the conference preparations to distract me from my woes and to provide an outlet for my continued desire to be productive. Three younger and, fortunately, healthier colleagues were integrally involved with me in preparations to arrange and direct the conference. Video presentations, which offer a wonderful medium for teaching complex surgical techniques, were to be a major feature. Seemingly endless hours were required between January and May to harvest clip after clip from a total of 217 instructional videos that we had gathered from the audio-visual libraries of major professional societies, as well as medical provider houses and even surgeons' private collections. We were determined to make our conference videos superb.

I coached my three colleagues thoroughly in conducting the rapid-fire, interactive discussions with the audience that would accompany presentation of the videos. We also made elaborate arrangements for tutorial and participatory sessions that would involve dissection of and practice surgery on the cadavers. In addition, I personally scoured the GYN literature of the previous five years, a tedious task, to accumulate a formidable aggregation of scientific papers (including my own) that would be provided to conference attendees in a one-inch-thick syllabus. I also organized two DVD's, each containing seven illustrated operations, for conference attendees to take home. Meals and refreshment breaks for the three days of the program had to be arranged, too. Lastly, we contacted and engaged multiple surgical supply houses to exhibit at the conference and help cover the staggering expense. I wanted to make certain that this, my final educational venture, would be both flawless and superlative.

Eventually, June arrived, and so did the cadavers. An audience of 200 eager and aspiring gynecologists also showed up for what I knew would be a unique, dynamic and complex instructional conference in state-of-the-art female pelvic surgery. The conference proved to be an enormous success. Every state, including Hawaii and Alaska, was represented. Attendees also came from Canada and Mexico. The cadaver-centered demonstrations sold out three weeks in advance. Enthusiasm remained at a fever pitch throughout the three days. I tried to be everywhere, in a wheelchair, no less, my faculty colleagues having observed that a walker was inefficient for traversing the various venues of the meeting. I reluctantly agreed, rationalizing that, if a president could run the country for 13 years from a wheelchair, I certainly could run a conference from one for three days. In the end, we received accolades and high marks from all.

For one who had so recently escaped death and who was also witnessing the final act of an impassioned career, it was a heady and emotion-laden experience. Dr. Jaffe had insisted on including the following dedication in the syllabus:

> The Department of Obstetrics and Gynecology of the Robert Wood Johnson Medical School—Camden and the Cooper University Hospital commemorate this gynecologic surgical conference to the illustrious career of Marvin H. Terry Grody, M.D. As he now moves from the active clinical and pedagogical medical sphere, he is seen by his peers, colleagues, and students as a master

> practitioner, surgeon, innovator, and teacher whose achievements and contributions will leave an everlasting imprint on their own careers. His tireless devotion, wit, sense of humor, enthusiasm, warmth, and pursuit of excellence will remain with us always.

At the conclusion of the conference, the audience graciously favored me with a warm and enthusiastic standing ovation, not the first but definitely the last of my 52-year career. It was immensely gratifying. My final achievement and contribution really had taken place. Quite often following my December 20th mishap, I had thought I would not make it, but I had!

How do I explain my survival and conference success? The answer to all good things for me has always been "Sue." She is and has been my life, my heart and my soul. She has made everything work for me. So now it was time for Sue. I vowed to catch up and, though I almost blew my timing, to finish my story with her.